Contents

Foreword by Alan Johnson

What is the best way to care for children who, for reasons not of their making, are unable to grow up with their birth parents? This is a crucial question for any civilised society, and I believe that the nature of the response is a test of how progressive and compassionate that society really is.

Care Matters proposes a set of answers to this question for us here in England in the first decade of the twenty first century. It starts from the premise that our goals for children in care should be exactly the same as our goals for our own children: we want their childhoods to be secure, healthy and enjoyable – rich and valuable in themselves as well as providing stable foundations for the rest of their lives.

Unfortunately, at the moment our care system fails to enable most children who enter it to achieve these aspirations. This is despite the efforts of many committed people – professionals and non-professionals alike – and the determination and resilience of the children themselves. This Green Paper shows that for many of the 60,000 children who are in care at any one time, childhood and adolescence are often characterised by insecurity, ill health and lack of fulfilment. This is terribly sad. And we can hardly be surprised that it results in many children in care underachieving educationally and getting nowhere near fulfilling their potential as adults.

Some may say that part of the reason for this is that children who enter care come disproportionately from poor backgrounds and have complex needs, but it is inexcusable and shameful that the care system seems all too often to reinforce this early disadvantage, rather than helping children to successfully overcome it.

It is not that policy and practice have stood still in recent years. Along with all other children, children in care have benefited from our radically transformed child care provision and education reforms since 1997, and from strengthened children's services through the *Every Child Matters* agenda. Children in care have also gained from a series of initiatives aimed at improving life in and beyond care, including the Quality Protects programme and the Children (Leaving Care) Act 2000.

Quite simply, it is now clear that this help has not been sufficient. The life chances of all children have improved but those of children in care have not improved at the same rate. The result is that children in care are now at greater risk of being left behind than was the case a few years ago – the gap has actually grown.

This is neither acceptable nor inevitable and we are determined through the proposals in this

Green Paper to first halt the trend and secondly to reverse it. Addressing every aspect of these children's lives and every public service they encounter, the Green Paper aims to transform both the way in which the care system works for children and the quality of experience they and others on the edge of entering or leaving care actually receive. And in doing this, we are determined to put the voice of the child in care at the centre both of our reforms and of day-to-day practice. It is only by listening to these children that we can understand their concerns and know whether or not we are meeting their needs.

These are ambitious but achievable aspirations provided that all of us with a role to play in central and local government, and in all other services across the public, private and voluntary sectors give these issues the focus and attention they need – not just now but relentlessly and consistently into the future.

I want to stress that this is a *Green* Paper and that we are genuinely interested in hearing views about our proposals. Will they make a difference to the lives of children in care – enough to achieve the transformation we want to see? If not, what more should we do? Please tell us.

The fact that children in care have to rely on the State for part or all of their upbringing makes them truly special. It is what distinguishes them from many others who also need extra help. It is why, in my view, we are under an urgent obligation to take action with them and for them.

At present the arrangements for caring for them are collectively referred to in legislation as the 'looked after system'. With the publication of this Paper I intend that in future, children in care will be properly cared for and supported, with the 'looked after system' living up to its name. I look forward to working with the many good people up and down the country who are committed to children in care and in a position to make a difference for them, and with the children themselves, to make sure this really happens.

Rt Hon Alan Johnson MP

Care Matters:
Transforming the Lives of Children and Young People in Care

Presented to Parliament
by the Secretary of State for Education and Skills
by Command of Her Majesty
October 2006

Cm 6932   £25.00

Executive Summary

Although outcomes for children in care have improved in recent years, there remains a significant and widening gap between these and the outcomes for all children. This situation is unacceptable and needs to be addressed urgently. This Green Paper sets out a radical package of proposals for change which will be delivered only through absolute commitment from central and local government and from professionals working on the front line. We have no doubt that this commitment exists.

In setting our priorities for change, we are driven by the knowledge that these are our children, and that the childhood we are giving them has not been good enough. We have an excellent legacy of achievement on which to build, and a dedicated workforce standing ready to deliver. The time has come to accelerate the pace of change, and to make care not only a way out of difficult situations at home, but a bridge to a better childhood and a better future.

The case for reform

1   Chapter 1 sets out the shocking statistics on the education of children in care. Only 11% of children in care attained 5 good GCSEs in 2005 compared with 56% of all children, and similar performance gaps exist at all ages both before and after Key Stage 4.

2   The long-term outcomes of children in care are also devastating. They are over-represented in a range of vulnerable groups including those not in education, employment or training post-16, teenage parents, young offenders, drug users and prisoners.

3   A lot of progress has been made for children over the last decade. We have seen an increase of eleven percentage points in the proportion of all young people gaining 5 A*-C GCSEs, and the proportion of young people in education, employment or training by 19 now stands at 87% – the highest it has ever been.

4   In the early years too, the dedication of local residents and professionals to the Sure Start agenda has contributed to a rise in registered childcare places to 1.26 million – almost double the level in 1997 – and the creation of 894 Children's Centres, offering services to over 715,000 children and their families.

5   We have also taken a range of steps to address directly the problems experienced by children in care, and progress has been

made through a number of reforms including:

- Quality Protects in 1998;

- The Care Standards Act 2000;

- The Prime Minister's adoption initiative;

- The Children (Leaving Care) Act 2000;

- The Social Exclusion Unit 2003 report on the Education of Children in Care; and

- The duty in the Children Act 2004 for local authorities to promote the education of children in care.

6　The outcomes of the 60,000 children in care at any one time have improved in recent years: the proportion gaining 5 A*-C GCSEs has risen from 7% in 2000 to 11% in 2005 and the proportion known to be participating in education, employment or training at age 19 has increased by 8% since 2002, when the Children (Leaving Care) Act 2000 came into effect. But it is clear that they are not improving at the same rate as those of all children.

7　Children in care are a group who are especially deserving of our help precisely because they are in care. As their corporate parent the State cannot and must not accept any less for them than we would for our own children.

Children on the edge of care

8　While most of the proposals in this Green Paper are aimed at children who are already in the care of the local authority, it is important also to recognise that many children come in and out of care in a short space of time, and several spend more than one period in care. Chapter 2 looks at the sorts of interventions which can help to prevent children needing to come into care in the first place, and to resettle them with their families after being in care where that is the best option for the child.

9　This means – in line with our reforms of children's services through the *Every Child Matters* programme – identifying problems early and responding to them quickly by offering sustained, multi-disciplinary support.

10　Our proposals include:

- New research on identifying and responding to neglect;

- Testing out a model of intensive whole-family therapy which aims to keep families together where possible;

- Improving the links between adults' and children's services in order to ensure that professionals working with either group see the family as a whole; and

- Creating a Centre of Excellence for Children's and Families Services[1] in order to identify and spread evidence-based solutions to the problems experienced by families whose children are on the edge of care.

11　Chapter 2 also launches a national debate on the future of care. We want to use the Green Paper to explore who care is for, whether there are any groups of children for whom care is not an appropriate response, and what we want the population of children in care to look like in the future.

1　As announced in *Reaching Out: An Action Plan on Social Exclusion*

The role of the corporate parent

12 Children have told us that the lack of a consistent adult in their lives is a major and harmful feature of being in care. Chapter 3 sets out in detail how the corporate parenting role should be carried out in order to address this gap.

13 Our proposals include:

- Exploring the feasibility of piloting new independent 'social care practices', small independent groups of social workers who contract with the local authority to provide services to children in care;

- Piloting the use of individual budgets for each child in care to be held by their lead professional – the social worker;

- Clarity over the role and use of care plans; and

- A revitalisation of the independent visitor scheme in order to provide 'independent advocates' for children in care.

Better placements

14 Evidence shows that frequent moves between care placements have a drastic effect on the ability of children and young people to succeed both in education and in other areas of their lives. Currently children in care are moved between placements far too frequently.

15 Chapter 4 sets out proposals radically to reform the placements system, improving the number and quality of foster carers and ensuring that children are only placed in residential children's homes which meet high standards of care.

16 Our proposals include:

- Introducing a tiered framework of placements to respond to different levels of need, underpinned by a new qualifications framework, fee structure and national minimum standards;

- Piloting for younger children the use of intensive foster care with multi-agency support;

- Improving the recruitment of foster carers through specially-tailored recruitment campaigns;

- Extending the use of specialist foster care for children with complex needs; and

- Introducing new regional commissioning units to secure better value for money and introduce placement choice for children.

A first class education

17 While the experiences they have in their placement are critical to children in care, the school environment and the way in which teachers and other school staff work with them are also vital to their chances of success. But many children in care currently have a poor experience of school: they tend to be in lower performing schools, be moved round between schools too often, and receive insufficient support within school to flourish.

18 Chapter 5 sets out how we will work with local authorities as corporate parents and with schools to secure the very best education for these children. We want to ensure that every child in care is in a good school, and is given the support they need to make the most of being in that school. We are committed to ensure that children

in care also fare well in our further education system.

19 Our proposals include:

- A 'virtual headteacher' in every local area responsible for driving up the performance of schools in relation to children in care;

- Providing local authorities with the power to direct schools to admit children in care, even where the school is fully subscribed;

- An enhanced entitlement to free school transport to ensure that where children do move placement they do not necessarily also need to change school;

- Better support in school to prevent exclusions of children in care; and

- A dedicated budget for each social worker to spend on improving the educational experience of every child in care.

Life outside school

20 This Green Paper is not only about the part which education and social services have to play in improving the lives of children and young people. It is truly a cross-Government agenda. Taking as its starting point the aim of securing for children in care the kind of happy, fulfilled childhood which we would want for our own children, the Green Paper also has a range of proposals for ensuring that children in care access all the other types of positive activities and support which children generally tend to enjoy.

21 Our proposals include:

- Encouraging local authorities to provide free access for children in care to all their facilities including leisure centres, sports grounds and youth clubs;

- A new model of comprehensive health provision for each child in care;

- Better training for a range of professionals including paediatricians on how to work with children in care;

- Improved access for children in care and their foster parents to Children's Centre provision; and

- Enhanced opportunities for them to participate in stimulating and rewarding personal development activities and volunteering.

The transition to adult life

22 We know that the long-term outcomes of many people who were in care as children are distressing: care leavers are over-represented in some of our most vulnerable groups of adults including young parents, prisoners, and the homeless. They are also under-represented in further and higher education, and the proportion of young people leaving care aged 19 without any form of purposeful activity such as employment, training or education is much higher than that of their peers.

23 This Green Paper signals a turning point in the way young people in care are treated as they grow older. We want to abandon a system where young people are forced to leave care as early as age 16. We want an approach which continues to support them as long as they need it, which ceases to talk about 'leaving care' and instead ensures that young people move on in a gradual, phased and above all prepared way.

24   Our proposals include:

- Piloting a veto for young people over any decisions about moving on from care before they turn 18;

- Piloting allowing young people to continue to live with foster carers up to the age of 21, receiving the support they need to continue in education;

- Providing a top-up to the Child Trust Funds of young people in care;

- Creating more supported accommodation for young people; and

- Introducing a national bursary for young people in care going to university.

Making the system work

25   We are confident that the proposals set out in this Green Paper will deliver a step change in the outcomes of children in care. But as the corporate parent of children in care we cannot rely on expectations alone: we need to take decisive action in instances of failure. Chapter 8 sets out a new accountability framework which works with the grain of the forthcoming Local Government White Paper to ensure that failure for this group of vulnerable children is identified and addressed.

26   Our proposals include:

- Asking Ofsted to carry out a regular inspection of how each local authority is meeting the educational needs of children in care;

- Introducing an annual national stock-take by Ministers of the progress of children in care;

- Expecting every local authority to set up a 'children in care council';

- Making Independent Reviewing Officers more independent; and

- Making the education of children in care one of the DfES's key national priorities for local government.

Next steps

27   We want to hear a range of views on this package of proposals – particularly those of children and young people who are or have been in care. We are offering a range of ways to take part in this consultation exercise, which runs from 9 October until 15 January. This will include conferences and events throughout the country as well as the setting up of working groups looking at:

- **The future of the care population;**

- **Social care practices;**

- **Placement reform; and**

- **Best practice in schools.**

28   We value your responses to this document highly and we will take into account the views which you give us during the consultation period. After the consultation we will publish an initial response, including a version for young people, in 2007. Final decisions on proposals with cost implications from 2008/09 onwards will be taken in the context of the 2007 Comprehensive Spending Review.

Chapter 1
The need for reform

Summary

A decade of investment and reform alongside commitment and enthusiasm at local level has made a huge difference to children. Together we have cut poverty, raised educational standards and improved the life chances of the most disadvantaged. But children in care are being left behind. Their attainment is not keeping pace with that of other children and the gap is growing wider. That cannot be allowed to continue. These are children for whom the state, as corporate parent, has a special responsibility and we must demand the same for them as we would for our own children. There are clear priorities for reform if we are to begin to close the gap in outcomes:

- Better support for those on the edge of the care system;

- Making sure there is a more consistent adult in each child's life to fulfil the State's responsibilities as corporate parent;

- Giving every child in care a stable, high quality placement;

- Getting every child in care a place in a good school, helping them to get the most out of it and supporting them to continue in education post-16;

- Securing support for all aspects of children's lives outside school;

- Supporting children better to make the transition into adult life; and

- Ensuring clear, strong accountability to make the whole system focus on the needs of children in care.

1.1 The state has a unique responsibility for children in care. It has taken on the task of parenting some of society's most vulnerable children and in doing so it must become everything a good parent should be. It must offer a nurturing home and a happy childhood, must be ambitious for children's futures, and must be demanding of schools and services to get the best for these children.

1.2 That ambition is one that is shared across the public services and is driven forward by committed professionals and carers working on the ground. Despite this, and despite change for the better for all children, the outcomes of children in care remain shockingly low. Far from being lifted on a rising tide of higher attainment for all, they are being left behind as the gap in educational outcomes grows wider. In this Green Paper we set out how we will create a step change for children in care. Our determination to do this is built on the ambitions of children in care themselves, who want no less than any other child.

" I want to be free of my past, better than my present and always ambitious for my future."

" People make assumptions on kids in the system – they all seem to get labelled as trouble makers."

Our pledge to children in care

1.3　However long or short a time children spend in care, it should make a positive difference to their lives. Many will enter care during a troubled part of their childhood when they are on a path towards poor qualifications and minimal prospects in adult life. Care must change that course, whether by helping settle a difficult family situation or by offering the child a stable new home through long term care, special guardianship or adoption.

1.4　We believe that to make this difference care must be a positive experience for children. It must raise their aspirations and offer better opportunities to enjoy childhood. We will use this Green Paper to make a pledge to all children to capture that ambition.

1.5　What every child needs will of course be different and we must have a system that responds to individual need, but there are some things we want for every child of a suitable age. We therefore want all local authorities to develop a **pledge for children in care**, which will set out those things that all children in their care will receive. Some local authorities already offer such a pledge to their children in care, and we would like to see this replicated nationwide.

1.6　We believe that there will be some things which should be at the core of the pledge offered by every local authority. These might include:

- **A choice, made with their social worker, of high quality placements;**

- **24/7 support from their social worker or an out of hours contact;**

- **A minimum entitlement to sport and leisure activities – for example, 4 hours a week;**

- **A chance to take part in volunteering;**

- **Twice yearly health assessments for under 5's and annual health assessments and twice yearly dental check ups for older children;**

- **An independent advocate;**

- **The choice of when to move on to enter adult life, up to the age of 18; and**

- **The right to have their voice heard and influence the work of the local authority through participation in a 'Children in Care Council'.**

1.7　There will be other things which local authorities will wish to consider including in their pledge – for example, giving older children in care a savings account. During the consultation period we will consider with children in care, local authorities and others which elements should form the core of every pledge and which elements are more likely to vary by local area.

Delivering change

1.8 The last decade has seen massive change for all children, and especially for those most in need. 800,000 children have been lifted out of poverty through our reforms of taxation and welfare. Reform in schools, and the efforts of teachers, have seen a welcome rise in school standards. A rise from 45% of children gaining 5 or more A*-C grades at GCSE in 1997 to 56% in 2005 offers greater life chances and a better future for thousands of children and young people.

1.9 More than ever before, local services are embracing a shared focus on children, putting an end to a culture in which families were forced to fit themselves around service boundaries instead of services fitting around them. *Every Child Matters*, which spells out our aim for every child to be healthy, stay safe, enjoy and achieve, make a positive contribution and achieve economic wellbeing, and the *Youth Matters* framework are offering young people a better chance to enjoy childhood and take an active part in their communities. In the early years too, the dedication of local residents and professionals to the Sure Start agenda has contributed to a rise in registered childcare places to 1.26 million – almost double the level in 1997 – and the creation of 894 Children's Centres offering services to over 715,000 children and their families.

1.10 The most vulnerable have always been at the heart of the change agenda. Quality Protects in 1998 set the standard, offering sustained investment of £885 million over five years. A renewed focus on the needs of these children, and an emphasis on listening to their views, led to greater stability in children's lives and far more being adopted from care.

1.11 Reforms such as the Children (Leaving Care) Act 2000 and the Prime Minister's initiative on adoption have also put children first. Children who would otherwise have had little to look forward to were offered a chance of happiness and success in later life. Over the last five years, 3,900 more children have been adopted than would have been if adoptions had remained at 1999-2000 levels. And the proportion of care leavers in education and employment at the age of 19 has risen from 46% in 2002 to 59% in 2005, while far more care leavers remain in touch with their local authority (an increase from 75% to 89% over the same period). The publication of *A Better Education for Children in Care* by the Social Exclusion Unit in 2003 led to further reform through the introduction of an explicit duty in the Children Act 2004 for local authorities to promote the educational outcomes of children in care; reforms to give children in care top priority for school admissions; and new guidance clarifying the roles of social workers, foster carers and school governors.

1.12 The Commission for Social Care Inspection (CSCI) report that children in care have seen a difference. Many now say that they are treated well, and believe that their lives

For **Kate**, being in care has made a real difference for the better. Kate entered care around the age of nine and is now nearly fifteen. Her parents died when she was very young, and she was looked after by her grandparents until they became unable to cope. She has learning difficulties and is on the autistic spectrum, something that was originally missed in the concerns about her grief. This, however, has not prevented a truly successful placement in care, with carers who plan to continue to care for Kate when she is an adult. According to her social worker Kate has 'superb foster carers' and a 'brilliant school' where she is taught in a small class with an approach geared to autistic children by a very committed teacher. There is a support package with an excellent community nurse and short breaks with a school support worker and there is further support from the carers' daughters who spend a lot of time with Kate.

have improved since becoming involved with social services. And the *Every Child Matters* reforms provide a new climate and a favourable framework on which to build.

But the gap in outcomes is getting wider

1.13 Despite all of this investment and reform and despite the work and commitment of local authorities, carers and social workers, the life chances of many children in care remain bleak. Especially in the light of the scale of investment in supporting children in care, it is unacceptable that their outcomes remain so poor. Between 2000-01

and 2004-05 total expenditure increased by around £230 million for children in residential care and by around £330 million for those in foster care, representing real terms increases of 20% and 44% respectively[2], while the care population only rose by 3% during that time. Over the same period, the proportion of children in care getting 5 good GCSEs rose by only 3 percentage points.

1.14 Children in care are a diverse group, with very different reasons for entering care and differing experiences of the system. Data shows that their outcomes are poor even

GCSE performance of children in care in year 11 compared with all children, twelve months ending 30 September

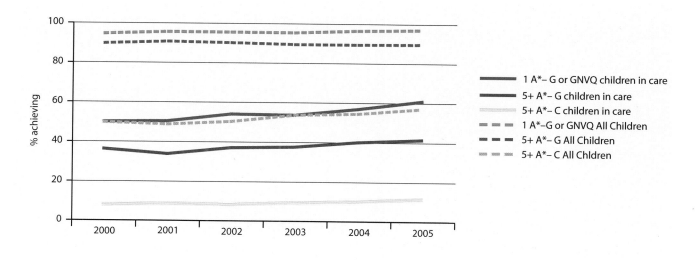

2   DfES data return: PSSEX1 http://www.ic.nhs.uk/pubs/persocservexp2005

when compared to other children with similar backgrounds and problems. GCSE attainment for children in care is not only far behind that of all children, but also significantly lower than that of children entitled to free school meals and those from deprived communities. Even when compared against children with similar levels of SEN, deprivation, and mobility, children in care do significantly worse. Out of school, they often fare poorly and are three times more likely to be cautioned or convicted of an offence than other children.

1.15 These data show that while we have been successful in raising the outcomes of children in care, the gap between children in care and other children gaining 5A*-C grades has not narrowed but has begun to widen as our reforms have driven up the attainment of all children. This and similar trends illustrate the complexity of the task we and our partners face.

1.16 Beyond school age, the picture is even worse.

- At the age of 19, only 19% of care leavers are in further education and 6% in higher education compared to 38% of all young people participating in one or the other;

- Young women aged 15 to 17 who have been in care are 3 times more likely to become teenage mothers than others of their age;

- Research suggests that around 27% of adult prisoners have spent time in care[3]; and

- Over 30% of care leavers are not in education, employment or training at age 19 compared to 13% of all young people.

1.17 Annex C provides more detail on these data.

Children in care are a diverse group with different needs

1.18 Children in care are far from a homogenous group and their various pathways through the system mean that the population is constantly changing. There are around 60,000 children in care at any one time, making up 0.5% of all children. But as many as 85,000 children will spend some time in care over the course of a year, with many entering and leaving the system very rapidly. And around half of all children who come into care will spend at least two separate periods in care during their lives. There has been an increase in the overall number of children in care not because more children are entering care – the numbers are decreasing – but because the average length of stay in the system is increasing.

1.19 This Green Paper uses the term 'children in care' to include all children being looked after by a local authority, including those subject to care orders under section 31 of the Children Act 1989 and those looked after on a voluntary basis through an agreement with their parents.

1.20 Children enter care at different points in their lives and our data show trends in the type of care experience associated with entering at particular times. For instance,

---

3   *Reducing Re-offending by ex-prisoners*, Social Exclusion Unit (2002)

Robbie is eleven years old. His difficulties began two years ago when his mother left home to live with a new partner. Both she and his father proved unable to manage Robbie separately, and Robbie came into a care following an enquiry by social services about possible physical abuse. In the two years since then Robbie has had four placements and two failed attempts at returning home, which the social worker now sees as unrealistic. Robbie says he liked all but one of his placements, although only the recent one has been able to manage his behaviour. He has been in this foster placement for about a year and loves it there. The carers have been able to manage Robbie 's behaviour much better, not least because of their other children who have become role models for Robbie. Robbie has regular counselling from a voluntary organisation, and takes part in activities such as Karate and gymnastics. He is still in touch with his birth family and gives his father a call every week and sees his mother and brother when he can.

around half of the 25% who enter at primary age do so on a voluntary basis. The largest group (40%) enter aged 10-15, often following a long history of problems. Children enter care for many different reasons ranging from abuse to a need to offer parents or children a short break because of severe disability.

1.21 Research[4] shows that around 29% of those entering care under 5 are referred to social services by health professionals while those aged 10 to 14 are more likely to be referred

by the police (21%) or schools (15%). Overall, the greatest proportion of referrals – around 30% – comes from non-professionals such as parents, children, relatives or friends, demonstrating the importance of involving family and friends in approaches to early intervention.

1.22 The majority of children in care entered care on a mandatory basis as a result of care orders made by the courts – 65% compared with 31% entering on a voluntary basis through agreement

Children in care at 31 March 2005 by category of need

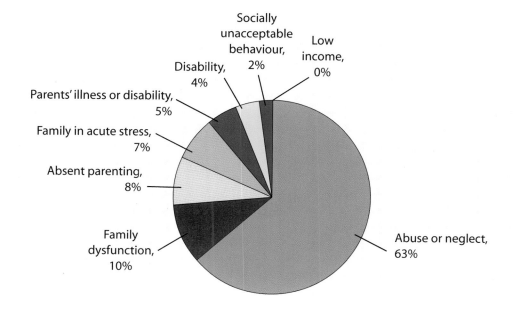

---

4   Cleaver, Walker and Meadows (2004): *Assessing Children's Needs and Circumstances*

between social services and their parents. There has been an increase in the proportion who are the subject of care orders.

1.23 Critically, we know that few children spend their whole childhood in care. 40% stay for under 6 months, and only 13% stay for 5 years or more. Consequently, support for birth families and managing a successful return home for the majority who go back to their families is crucial.

1.24 Of those who do return home, we know that many come back into care. Around half have more than one period in care during their childhood. Again, this suggests the importance of a well managed return home.

1.25 Children in care are ethnically diverse, and research shows that they will benefit from care which reflects this diversity[5]. Black and mixed race children are over-represented (each comprises 3% of all children, but 8% of those in care) and Asian children are under-represented (6% of all children, but 3% of those in care).

1.26 In addition, around 3,000 unaccompanied asylum seeking children are cared for by local authorities at any one time. This group of children often have different needs to other children in care, which will be looked at in more detail in a forthcoming consultation to be published by the Home Office.

1.27 Our strategy must also reflect children's different experiences of care and the differences between placements. 68% are in foster care; 13% are in residential care;

and about 9% are placed with their families with the rest placed for adoption or in a variety of more specialist placements.

1.28 This level of diversity both in the population and in children's experiences of care shows that we cannot offer a one-size-fits-all solution to closing the gap in outcomes. Consequently, the proposals we set out in this Green Paper aim to address a wide range of issues and take a flexible approach so that responses can be tailored to the needs of individual children.

The barriers to attainment

1.29 Many of the issues we have outlined have been hard to tackle for decades, and lasting solutions have proved elusive. Yet children in care should benefit from rising attainment in schools and better life chances every bit as much as other children do. In the remainder of this chapter we examine the key barriers to narrowing the gap and in the light of that analysis set out our priorities for reform.

Problems resulting from pre-care experiences

1.30 Research shows that maltreated children are far less likely to form secure attachments and that there are links between early neglect and physiological brain development[6]. Given that 63% of children in care are there as a result of abuse or neglect, it is likely that the high incidence of mental health problems in the care population, and the high frequency of placement breakdown, is in many cases a result of pre-care experiences.

---

5   Barn (2006): *Improving Services to Meet the Needs of Minority Ethnic Children and Families (Quality Protects Research Briefing 13)*

6   Glaser (2000): *Child Abuse and Neglect and the Brain – A Review*

1.31 To address this we must improve our approach to interventions directed at children at risk of needing to come into care and their families by building on approaches that have proven successful at local level.

There is no consistent person able to act as an engaged parent

1.32 Most children have contact with a range of professionals in the course of their childhood, but for the majority this is managed by their parents, who understand and respond to all aspects of their children's lives.

1.33 For children in care the day to day responsibility of parenting is divided between carers and the social worker representing the local authority as corporate parent. However, there are high rates of turnover among social workers and staff in children's homes, and a lack of stability in children's placements means that many children lack a consistent adult in their lives. In addition, organisational structures in local authorities can result in responsibility for children being passed from one part of the organisation to another during their time in care. Whilst many children in care receive an excellent service, far too many do not.

" I don't know who my social worker is at the minute, it would be nice to have a permanent one."[7]

1.34 We need to explore how we can encourage a more consistent lead professional role with one person

remaining consistently in a child's life and staying with them as far as possible throughout their time in care and beyond.

Placements do not always meet children's needs

1.35 There are strong links between positive parenting and educational outcomes.[8] The quality of support received in placements is therefore fundamental to the outcomes of children in care. There are some excellent placements, and there is no doubt that both foster and residential carers are committed to the children they care for.

1.36 However, despite this dedication, far too many placements are not meeting children's needs. Only around 25% of care homes are meeting 90% or more of the National Minimum Standards. Qualification levels of staff tend to be poor, and only 23% of residential care staff are qualified to the expected standard for these settings.[9]

1.37 Fostering services have similar problems. Over a third fail to meet National Minimum Standards on suitability to work with children and one in four fail to meet the standard on providing suitable carers. A high level of placement instability and frequent breakdowns suggest that many children are not in the right placement for them or are not receiving sufficient support.

1.38 The analysis set out in Chapter 4 also shows that we are not currently achieving value for money from our spending on placements. And a lack of strategic commissioning is leading in many

---

7   This quote and others in the Green Paper are from children in care and were provided by the Children's Rights Director

8   Deforges (2003): *The impact of parental involvement, parental support and family education on pupil attainment*

9   The State of Social Care in England 2004-05, Commission for Social Care Inspection (2005)

instances to children being placed wherever a bed is available rather than in the best home for them, pointing to a need to improve the planning and commissioning of placements.

Children in care are not getting the best from schools

1.39 As well as the care-related factors listed above, we know that children in care are less likely to be placed in high performing schools whether measured in terms of absolute performance or value added.

1.40 Further problems arise from the way in which the care and education systems interact. Frequent placement changes and a high rate of exclusions mean that children in care are five times more likely than other children to move school in years 10 or 11, a major factor affecting exam performance.[10] Research, and our conversations with children, also show that foster carers often attribute little importance to schooling and that schools often fail to understand the needs of children in care.[11]

II My maths teacher told my whole class that I'm in care.*II*

1.41 To address barriers to higher achievement in schools we must ensure that children in care are able to get into the right school, make sure they stay there once they are in, and help them get the best out of their time there.

Children need better support to access the right services out of school

1.42 Children in care have a broader range and higher level of need than other children. It is particularly important that they can access a full range of services from schools, GPs, hospitals and other local agencies.

1.43 However, around one in five children in care do not receive annual health checks and they are significantly more likely than other children to become teenage parents or commit criminal offences – though the numbers in each group remain small – suggesting that children's needs are not being met.

II Some come into care because of problems that aren't to do with them, but they end up with their own problems and a criminal record.*II*

1.44 We need to understand how all partners in local children's trusts (local partnerships introduced through *Every Child Matters*) can fulfil their responsibilities to children and young people in care to support a well-rounded life and enjoyment of positive activities in and out of school and into adulthood.

Children are not being helped to make a smooth transition to adult life

1.45 Despite the success of reforms such as the Children (Leaving Care) Act 2000 the longer term life outcomes of children in care remain poor. In 2005 28% of care leavers were aged 16, and those in

---

10 School Census. The data collected through the School Census is thought to under report numbers of children in care and should therefore be treated with caution.

11 Sinclair (2005) *Fostering Now: Messages from Research*

residential care were most likely to leave at 16. This is compared with an average age of leaving care of 24 for all young people. Many young people find themselves entering adult life too early and research shows that they do so ill-equipped for adult life and with very little long term support.

" In a children's home I had loads of security, [leaving care] was all change and too much. "

1.46 We need to support a smoother transition to independence if the gap in long-term outcomes is to close. We need to offer young people a greater voice in how and when they enter adult life and ensure continuity of support after they do so to help them adjust.

1.47 Disabled young people and their families often find the transition to adulthood both stressful and difficult. For many, there has been a lack of co-ordination between the relevant agencies and little involvement from the young person. Some young people are not transferred from children's to adults' services with adequate care plans, which can result in their exclusion from adult services. In addition, some disabled young people experience a decline in the services they receive. This can lead to a regression in their achievement and/or a deterioration in their condition.

Accountability is not clear or strong enough

1.48 The accountability mechanisms that exist in the current system are very limited. Only the local authority is formally accountable for the outcomes of children in care and even their accountability is weak.

1.49 Inspection reports tend to be at a high level with little focus on the reasons for outcomes and there is no statistical link between the star ratings local authorities receive in inspections and the outcomes of children in their care. It is likely that part of the problem arises from the comparatively small numbers of these children which mean they can be invisible in the management information used by local authorities and in school performance tables.

1.50 We will be successful in transforming the outcomes of children in care only if we succeed in addressing this and in delivering a system that makes clear the role of everyone at each level of that system, the mechanisms to hold them to account, and what will happen in cases of failure.

Questions for consultation

Are the elements we suggest for our 'pledge' the right ones?

Are there any other key barriers to attainment which we should address in order to transform outcomes?

Chapter 2
Children on the edge of care

Summary

Few children want to come into care. Even those who have been through abuse or neglect usually continue to love their families and want to remain with them. We must have no hesitation about bringing children into care where safeguarding or other concerns mean that is the right thing to do. But children should be supported in their families unless it is against their interests for them to be. This means identifying problems early and responding quickly by offering sustained, multi-disciplinary support. Our proposals include:

- Publishing new research on identifying neglect early and effectively, and offering a training resource for practitioners on how to do this;

- Evaluating the effectiveness of Family Functional Therapy;

- Issuing guidance to health and social care providers on effective practice in joint working between adult and children's services;

- Exploring the implications of and models for extending access to the Integrated Children's System (ICS), on a "read-only" basis, to partners outside the local authority such as schools and health services;

- Creating a Centre of Excellence for Children's and Family Services to deliver a systematic approach to sharing best practice;

- Promoting the use of Family Group Conferencing through a programme of national events and training; and

- Establishing a working group on the future of care to set a clear vision for the next ten to fifteen years centred on our determination to support children in their families where possible.

2.1 Children have told us that more should be done to prevent the need for care and help them stay with their families. Bringing children into care is a huge and often traumatic step for them and the families they leave behind, and should happen only where it is right for the child.

2.2 There is no doubt that care will always be the right option for some children, for whom staying with their family could be

We are working with 14 pathfinder areas which are piloting models of **targeted youth support** (TYS) to enable institutions to identify problems and respond quickly. TYS is an example of *Every Child Matters* in action for young people, reflecting the specific needs and circumstances of teenagers. TYS will work to support the resilience of young people and equip them with the personal and social resources they need to ensure their wellbeing and positive futures. TYS addresses a wide range of issues relevant to vulnerable young people including careers information and guidance, substance misuse, mental health support, family planning advice, accommodation and risky behaviours. We are committed to supporting full-roll out by April 2008. This will make a significant contribution to preventing children needing to come into care and supporting them better on their return home from care.

dangerous or damaging to their welfare. Where this is the case, those children should enter care quickly and receive excellent support. But there is undoubtedly more we could do to help many children and their families cope with difficult situations so that the child can stay at home. It is also vital that parental responsibility is recognised in all circumstances and that parents are supported to help them fulfil their responsibilities to their children.

" All children should have time with their families, even if watched.*"*

2.3 We should concentrate our efforts on avoiding the need for care, except for those who truly need its support. We must identify problems earlier and respond quickly and effectively. And our responses must be driven by what we know are the key characteristics of effective interventions:

- Multi-disciplinary and multi-agency;

- Centred around the child;

- Sustained, with support continuing as long as it is needed; and

- Evidence based, grounded in robust evaluation of what works.

2.4 The *Every Child Matters* and *Youth Matters* programmes are leading to an unprecedented level of reform across children's services. Many local areas are putting into place a "whole-system" approach where the needs of children, young people and families are supported by flexible services which can respond to different levels of need.

2.5 This is supporting a shift of focus away from managing short-term crises and towards an increasing emphasis on prevention and supporting children and young people in their families. We know that this practice is effective and data from local authorities shows that those who support a higher proportion of children in their families, instead of in care, consistently receive higher star ratings in inspections.

2.6 It is essential that services are delivered in a way which families feel comfortable with. There is no point in developing an excellent service which children and families are unwilling to take up. Research shows for instance that different approaches are needed for different sections of the community and that families from black and minority ethnic backgrounds will not

Helen (now six years old) is at home. She spent four months in care last year as the result of domestic violence and neglect. Her father abused amphetamines and this fuelled his violence. Helen sees things differently. She feels that she was in care to give her mum a rest. Helen thought it was a good idea that she came into care, and liked both her foster carers.

The plan from the beginning was that Helen should return home once her parents' problems had been addressed. While Helen was in care, her father stopped his substance abuse, and Helen was able to go home. She is still on the child protection register but her family and her social worker agree that the current situation is a good outcome for her.

take up services unless they are made more accessible to them[12].

Identifying risks and problems early

2.7 In the past, we have not been good enough at identifying problems quickly so that the need for care can be prevented. And yet there is clear evidence that early identification can help us to predict where problems will arise. In February 2005 there were 313,300 children in need supported in their families or independently by local authorities. We know that those who are in need[13] as a result of abuse or neglect are far more likely to enter the care system than those who are categorised as being in need for other reasons – around 30% of this group will enter care during their childhood.

2.8 But despite what we know about these and other predictive factors our responses have not been effective enough. Research shows that practitioners sometimes fail to identify neglect because of the absence of a specific incident that triggers intervention[14]. The findings of Serious Case Reviews in some areas have also revealed that our expectations of the care children from deprived backgrounds receive are not nearly high enough.

Merton have developed a successful approach to children's services, underpinned by a strategy setting out their strong belief that children should be supported in their families wherever possible. They have a range of services in place including short-term targeted family support services, parenting classes, family group conferences and written agreements with families. Services are designed specifically so that interventions can be put in place at short notice where a need is identified. These services help avoid the need to bring children into care, coupled with a system in which there is senior level oversight of any decision to accommodate a child or begin care proceedings. Merton have seen real successes, with a fall in the numbers of children in care from 220 in 2001 to only 117 by January 2006. Those who are in care are receiving strong support, described by the Commission for Social Care Inspection (CSCI) as "providing the best possible child care."

12   Thoburn et al. (2005) *Child Welfare Services for Minority Ethnic Families: The Research Reviewed*

13   "Children in Need" are defined by the Children Act 1989 as those whose health or development (whether physical, emotional, or intellectual) may be impaired, or limited without the provision of extra support, or who are disabled.

14   Jowitt (2003) *Policy and Practice in Child Welfare: Literature Review Series 3. Child Protection and the Decision-Making Process: Assessments of Risk and Systems of Professional Knowledge, Judgement and Beliefs*

2.9 We must be more ambitious than this. We need to take steps to identify risks much earlier, especially in cases of neglect which put children at a higher risk of needing to enter care. We have commissioned further research on the identification of neglect, and will:

- **Develop a training resource for practitioners drawing on the conclusions of that research.**

A multi-disciplinary approach

2.10 However, knowing how to identify problems will not be enough. Tragic cases such as that of Victoria Climbié have shown that a lack of effective working between professionals can lead to terrible outcomes which could have been avoided.

2.11 The Information Sharing Index, being developed for implementation by 2008, will provide a tool to support better communication among practitioners across education, health, social care and youth offending teams. The index will allow practitioners to contact each other more easily where they need to share information about children and young people who may need extra support.

2.12 The Index will hold only basic identification data about all children. For children in care and other children in need who are receiving services from their local authority, a more comprehensive information handling system is required. The Integrated Children's System (ICS) will provide this and is currently being rolled out nationally.

2.13 The ICS offers a means for practitioners to access and share key information about children in need or in care, and to manage caseloads more effectively. Once fully in place, the ICS will provide front line staff and their managers with a tool to record, collate, and analyse information on the needs of particular children, the interventions they have received, and plans for their future care. In order to ensure that the ICS maximises the benefit it can offer to children in care, we will:

- **Build the key components of the ICS and the Children Act legislative framework into the Social Work degree and the post-qualifying framework;**

- **Explore the implications of and models for extending access to the ICS, on a "read-only" basis, to those such as schools and health services who might be able to use the information to join up their approaches in supporting children. In considering this approach, we will evaluate practice in areas which**

NCH provide a Crisis Intervention service in which they offer a range of interventions to prevent the need for care. Interventions are developed to respond to local needs, in partnership with local authorities and other agencies in the local area. The interventions take many different forms but all are designed to build on strengths within families and targeted where there is a high risk of family breakdown. A team of experienced, skilled practitioners drawn from a range of backgrounds works with the family to help prevent the risk of care or to help manage a successful return home. In one NCH project, results for the first year of operation showed that 76 per cent of young people referred to the service did not enter the care system.

have already extended access to the ICS in this way.

2.14 Research[15] has found that in initial child protection conferences there is evidence of domestic violence in 50% of cases and substance misuse in 25%, demonstrating a history of problems in many of these families.

2.15 We are working to give professionals the autonomy they need to respond rapidly and in close partnership with one another. Recent changes have improved GP training and given them greater independence to commission and fund support directly. This is enabling them to co-ordinate a multi-disciplinary approach to care and to focus on the whole family, including the impact of adults' needs on children. But we know that there are still too many cases where the needs of the whole family are not considered when responding to an individual problem.

2.16 We need to improve the way in which adults' and children's services work together, recognising that the problems of adults can have a damaging impact on their families. This requires an approach which responds to the needs of the whole family, not only to individuals within it, and requires agencies to work closely together. For instance, given the high incidence of

parental substance misuse, it is important that Drug Action Teams (DATs) and children's services set joint local targets about how to work closely together. We also know that there is a very high incidence of parental mental health problems in the families of children at risk of coming into care. As a result, it is essential that the commissioning strategies of adult social care services and Primary Care Trusts respond to the needs of vulnerable parents. Therefore, we will:

- **Through the Commissioning Framework due for publication in December 2006 describe how PCTs can work with local authorities to strengthen local strategic needs assessment, with a particular focus on meeting the needs of vulnerable groups; and**

- **Publish joint evidence-based guidelines, through the Social Care Institute for Excellence and National Institute for Clinical Excellence, for adults' and children's health and social care services on parental mental health and child welfare. The guidelines will be based on a systematic review of research and existing practice in supporting parents with mental health problems and their children.**

St Helens has developed a 'universal home contact schedule' to give a consistent approach to services across all of St Helens' children's centres. The schedule sets out core expectations of when services such as health visiting will take place for all children from pre-birth to five. It also offers a framework for consistent additional support, joining up services such as midwifery, health visiting, oral health, and speech and language therapy. All families are given a named link worker to co-ordinate the service they receive from the first point of contact, which usually takes place 6–7 months before the child's birth.

---

15 Cleaver (2006) *The Impact of Domestic Violence and Substance Misuse on Children*

2.17 In the White Paper *Our Health Our Care Our Say* we made a commitment to develop a common assessment framework (CAF) for adults with complex and/or long term conditions whose care is best managed between primary health services and adult social care. As part of the development of the CAF for adults we will:

- **Explore the benefits of a co-ordinating role akin to the 'lead professional' working across health services and adults' social care for adults with complex or long-term needs.**

2.18 As *Reaching Out: An Action Plan on Social Exclusion* made clear, vulnerable adults often have a complex range of problems including offending behaviour, substance misuse and long-term physical and mental health problems, and can be receiving support from a number of different agencies and services. The Social Exclusion Task Force has been established to co-ordinate action across Government to help socially excluded groups. As part of its work it will develop, pilot and evaluate new approaches to improving outcomes for vulnerable adults and their families. For example, ten demonstration pilots are being set up to test evidence-based intensive parenting support delivered by health visitors and community midwives linked to Sure Start Children's Centres. To underpin these developments, and to help local areas improve links between children's and adults' services, we propose to:

- **Ensure the Social Exclusion Task Force considers how we can better meet the needs of parents with a complex range of problems and ensure they do not impact on their children.**

2.19 There is much still to do to build up our knowledge of the kind of interventions that will be most effective in supporting whole families. Functional Family Therapy is an intensive one-to-one programme which uses family therapists to support children in their families. The approach works both with families where children may be at risk of entering care and with those returning home.

2.20 The model is currently used mainly as a short term intervention with young people between the ages of 11 and 18. Up to 30 hours of direct services are provided over a three month period, ranging from clinical sessions to telephone discussions, working with each family member both separately and together to bring about a change in behaviour. We propose to:

- **Evaluate the effectiveness of Family Functional Therapy.**

The importance of a sustained intervention

2.21 Even the very best interventions will work only if they continue as long as they are needed. Far too often the competing demands on professionals mean that they will offer a short term response to a problem, just enough to calm a situation down, before having to move on to the next crisis. That approach is not working. Children can find themselves moving in and out of care because the support given to them and their family is not sustained once they return home.

" When you're going back to your family it should be step-by-step but they sent me back with no warning. I had an argument with my Mum and ended up homeless for 2 weeks."

2.22 Only 25% of children in a recent study had contact with their social worker after returning home from care[16]. At a time when around half of all children in care have more than one period in care during their childhood, it makes no sense to offer this limited kind of support.

2.23 We want to build on our knowledge of the kind of interventions that work best for children and can offer a long term solution for them and their families. The Respect Action Plan announced a range of measures aimed at increasing the quantity and quality of parenting programmes. The National Academy for Parenting Practitioners will support and deliver training for staff to deliver these programmes and a series of pathfinders will examine the issues related to widescale implementation of parenting programmes which have proved effective in trials – Webster/Stratton, Positive Parenting Programme and Strengthening Families/Strengthening Communities.

Interventions based on evidence

2.24 There is a host of innovative practice in this country and elsewhere. Local service providers are increasingly focusing their efforts on providing cross-disciplinary, sustained support for families, responding to better techniques for identifying problems early. Many of these approaches make a big difference to families, but suffer from a lack of evaluation. Even those that are proven to be effective are often used only in isolated areas while others may be casting around for the same solution.

2.25 We need to get better at systematically identifying the very best practice, drawn from robust evaluation of what really works for children including what works in engaging hard to reach sections of the community. We know that in other fields, including health, organisations such as the National Institute for Clinical Excellence have achieved a great deal by identifying and sharing knowledge of what is and is

The Dundee Families Project works with families who are at risk of eviction as a result of anti-social behaviour with the aim of tackling the underlying causes, addressing their challenging behaviour and ensuring they are able to sustain a tenancy. The work of the Project can help to prevent the breakdown of vulnerable families and assist with the rehabilitation of families where children have been looked after. The Project takes a holistic approach to family difficulties and offers a range of services through individual and couple counselling, family support and group work and balances this with the threat of enforcement action if the behaviour fails to change. Families housed in the residential unit are provided with 24-hour support and supervision. Staff run after-school and young people's group activities, while groups for adults cover cookery, parenting skills, anger management and tenancy issues.

A 2001 evaluation of the project indicated that, in Dundee alone, it saved £117,600 a year by preventing further problems for families. Earlier this year we announced in the Respect Action Plan that this approach would be rolled out nationwide through the establishment of a national network of intensive Family Intervention Projects.

---

16   Sinclair (2005) *Fostering Now: Messages from Research*

not effective, giving a nationally recognised seal of approval to what works. We will therefore explore the merits of:

- **Creating a national centre for excellence in children's and family services to deliver a systematic approach to sharing best practice across children's services.[17]**

2.26 The Centre would build on the work of the existing Social Care Institute for Excellence and the Centre for Excellence in Residential Child Care, but would look more widely and systematically to gather, evaluate and share information on successful and innovative approaches across the breadth of children's services.

2.27 The role of the centre would be to:

- Gather and review emerging research and evaluation both nationally and internationally, maintain a database of effective practice, and commission new research in key areas;

- Disseminate the knowledge it obtains to commissioners to ensure that they are able to focus resources on programmes and practice with a track record of effectiveness; and

- Disseminate knowledge to practitioners to build evidence-based practice which is responsive to the needs of and improves outcomes for children and families.

2.28 We would encourage service commissioners in all local areas to make use of the Centre's recommendations and services. In building up the knowledge base that would inform the Centre, we must

continue our commitment to funding the evaluation of pilots of specific approaches, based on what we know works.

The importance of family and friends

2.29 However excellent the range of interventions that is delivered, and however early problems are caught, there will always be cases where children cannot be cared for by their parents alone. Sometimes this means that children will need to enter full-time care. In other cases though it may be possible for care to be shared with other members of the family or with close friends. We believe that this is much better for most children than entering care, and children have told us they believe the same.

" Social services should ask every single person in my family if they could look after me but they only asked my Nan. "

2.30 But we know that family and friends are not the option of first resort often enough. One study found that 86% of family and friends placements were initiated by family members, not by the social worker[18]. We want to change this culture, and will:

- **Require local authorities to lodge with the court at the outset of care proceedings an outline plan for permanence for the child, which they are already required to draw up later in the course of care proceedings. This will provide greater clarity, and at an earlier stage, to all concerned. If a child is not to be supported by family or friends,**

---

17   As announced in *Reaching Out: An Action Plan on Social Exclusion*

18   Farmer and Moyers (2005) *Children Placed with Family and Friends: Placement Patterns and Outcomes*

the plan must make clear why this is not appropriate.

2.31 Research shows that placements with family and friends often lead to greater stability. In one study[19], 72% of placements with family and friends were still stable after two years of care compared to 55% of those with unrelated foster carers.

2.32 Family Group Conferencing can offer an effective way of finding alternatives to care within the family circle. Under this model social workers organise group discussions with family and friends of the child to consider alternative arrangements for their care to bring together the full resources of the family. International research has shown that Family Group Conferencing is effective in involving families and minimising the need for care for children from black and ethnic minority backgrounds[20].

2.33 We want to encourage the use of this approach to help secure the best possible care for children and will:

- **Promote the use of Family Group Conferencing through a programme of national events and training.**

2.34 We will do this through a series of events including:

- A national conference to promote the merits of Family Group Conferencing and launching a toolkit on its use for local authorities;

- Encouraging all authorities to nominate local co-ordinator posts, with the opportunity to shadow existing co-ordinators to build their skills and knowledge of the process; and

- Development and provision of specialist training for co-ordinators.

Where care is the right option

2.35 However good the interventions offered to families, there will always be cases where the best thing for the child is to enter care, particularly where there are safeguarding concerns. Local authorities take many different approaches to managing this process, and an essential area of practice which we want to examine further is identifying the approaches that yield the best outcomes for children. Some, for instance, delegate decisions about initiating care proceedings to social workers and their immediate managers, while others set in place much higher level scrutiny to ensure the decision is the right one.

2.36 We believe that any decision to bring children into care represents such a major

South Tyneside Council has expanded its Community Family Support Service using resources from the Children's Fund, allowing weekend and evening access to the team and quick responses to referrals – Family Group Conferencing is one of the approaches taken by the service to help children remain with their family. South Tyneside estimate that 92% of young people using the service during its first year of operation would have entered care had the service not been in place.

---

19 Farmer and Moyers (2005) *Children Placed with Family and Friends: Placement Patterns and Outcomes*

20 *Family Group Decision-making: Protecting Children and Women*, Pernell and Burford (2000)

Leicestershire has a number of accommodation panels who consider and challenge proposals to bring children in to care. The panels have an independent chair who is also responsible for management of the family support team. That team is able to offer intensive packages of support to a family in crisis, which may provide a means to keep the child supported effectively in their family.

step that there should always be senior level involvement in decision making. It is absolutely crucial though that doing so does not introduce delay in the process to the detriment of the child.

2.37 There are long-standing concerns that processes such as local authority decision making and the nature of the court system can leave children hanging in limbo at a time when more than anything they need certainty about their future. We are committed to addressing this by implementing the recommendations of the recent joint review of child care proceedings by the Department for Education and Skills and Department of Constitutional Affairs, including that:

- All safe and appropriate alternatives should be explored before court proceedings are started. In some cases this might include placement with other family members or providing support through Family Group Conferences to discuss all aspects of the family situation;

- Guidance and best practice on case preparation should be written up in one document for use by all local authorities; and

- The case management process in courts should be improved.

2.38 We know that parental substance misuse is often a factor in children needing to come

into care. The Advisory Council on the Misuse of Drugs report, *Hidden Harm*[21], estimated that there are between 250,000 and 350,000 children of drug users. Similarly, local research in three central London Boroughs identified that over 60% of cases in care proceedings involved parental substance misuse as a key issue.

2.39 Improvements to the way in which adults' and children's services work together, discussed above, are vital in responding to the needs of children of substance misusers. And a new toolkit, *Adult Drug Problems, Children's Needs*, developed by the National Children's Bureau and funded by the DfES, will help social workers in this area.

2.40 Given the high incidence of drug misuse in care proceedings, we also want to explore ways in which support for substance misusing parents can be brought together with care proceedings. We propose to:

- **Encourage local pilots of specialised family drug and alcohol courts, building on known good practice.**

2.41 Pilots will test a whole family approach through the courts, designed to bring together the care proceedings framework with services for substance misusing parents to improve outcomes for both children and adults.

---

21 Hidden Harm: Responding to the needs of children of problem drug users, Advisory Council on the Misuse of Drugs (June 2003)

The future of care

2.42 Intervening earlier and better to keep children in their families will change the nature of care. It will hopefully take us towards a smaller population of children in care, with only those most in need of its support entering care.

2.43 We know that younger children are more likely to enter care as the result of abuse or neglect and that they are particularly vulnerable to long-term impairment as a consequence of this pre-care experience. We have also had reports that older children, particularly with severe behavioural difficulties, sometimes enter care because their family feel unable to cope, even where support in their family might be a better option.

2.44 Now is the time to begin a debate on a new approach to care. We need a clear, long-term vision of how our reforms will build a sustained approach to supporting children and families before, during and after spending time in care. We believe that this vision will take us towards a situation in which:

- There are fewer children in the system overall;

- A proportion would continue to spend time in care on a very short-term, voluntary basis as part of supporting children in their families;

- Children who are the subject of care orders will be those who are unlikely to return home and so will be likely to stay for longer, or go on to be adopted;

- There is a continued increase in the use of adoption; and

- The average age of children in care will be younger as the family difficulties which bring in many older children are better addressed.

2.45 We now want to begin a national debate on what our long-term vision for the care system should be, looking beyond the proposals in this Green Paper by horizon scanning and considering what our strategy should be for the next 15-20 years. We will:

- **Establish a working group to consider this issue and to report in Spring 2007. Its report will inform our long-term strategy for supporting children both within and outside the care system. It will also be linked to an assessment of future trends in social exclusion and inequality.**

Questions for consultation

What more can be done to reassert the responsibility of parents and help them to fulfil those responsibilities?

Do you agree that there is a need for a more systematic approach to sharing effective practice in children's services? If so, how can we ensure maximum impact on supporting evidence-informed commissioning and practice?

What more could be done to support links between adults' and children's services, particularly in relation to substance misuse and mental health support?

What more could be done to support family and friends carers?

Is it right for us to work towards an increase in the number of children supported in families and, as a result, a smaller, younger care population with more complex needs?

Chapter 3
The role of the corporate parent

Summary

As the corporate parent of children in care the State has a special responsibility for their wellbeing. Like any good parent, it should put its own children first. That means being a powerful advocate for them to receive the best of everything and helping children to make a success of their lives.

Children's social workers embody the corporate parenting role on a day to day basis, but high turnover rates mean they are often an inconsistent parent. They can also lack the autonomy to be a strong advocate for the child. We want to change this and help social workers fulfil the role of an excellent corporate parent. Our proposals include:

- Piloting a model of 'social care practices': small groups of social workers holding individual budgets and commissioning placements for children in care, wholly independent of local authorities;

- Building on our existing pilots of budget-holding lead professionals to see how effective the role can be for children in care;

- Issuing revised guidance to all local authorities making clear how care plans should be prepared, used and maintained and what their contents should be, including requiring them to set out long term ambitions; and

- Building on the existing independent visitor scheme to provide independent advocates to act as mentors and advocates for children in care.

3.1 Entering care represents a significant change in a child's life. The State takes on an immense responsibility for these children by agreeing to undertake the parental role on a day to day basis. That means that all those working for the State at a local level – every councillor, every Director of Children's Services, every social worker or teacher – should demand no less for each child in care than they would for their own children.

3.2 What children need more than anything is a stable, confident parent able and willing to be vocal on their behalf. This is the role of their social worker but children have told us that this does not always happen well enough in practice. One message consistently at the top of children's priorities is that they want social workers who stay the same and are accessible to them.

" As soon as I get to know my social worker I get given a new one. "

People around the child

3.3 Children in care come into contact with a host of professionals and unless they are helped to manage this, the number of people in their lives can feel confusing and chaotic to them.

3.4 Any child, depending on their needs, and at different times in their lives, may find themselves in contact with doctors, teachers, speech and language therapists, learning mentors, Connexions personal advisers and many others. For the majority of children and young people this is simply a fact of life and is managed smoothly for them by their parents. It is the parents who

find out who to contact, make appointments, and demand the best service on their children's behalf.

3.5 Children in care, who often need help from a greater range of professionals than most other children, need their carers and social workers to take on this task. *Every Child Matters* introduced the role of a lead professional responsible for co-ordinating professionals in a team around the child so that children's needs are met smoothly instead of having to struggle to navigate a complex system.

3.6 The lead professional role may be taken on by a range of front line professionals including, for example, health workers and teachers. For children in care, however, the lead professional will almost always be the social worker because of the particular statutory responsibilities associated with them and so we refer to social workers rather than lead professionals throughout this document.

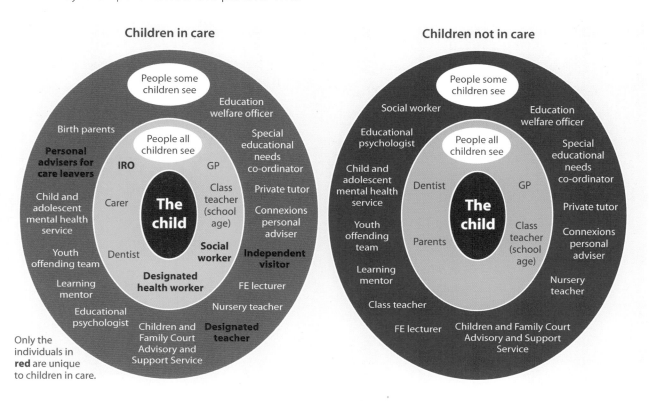

3.7 The diagram above illustrates the full range of people with whom children may find themselves in contact, and sets out how this differs for children in care. As it shows, there are very few people every child will see irrespective of their age and needs and comparatively few who children in care might see but others would not.

3.8 However, the key difference is the lack of clarity for children in care as to who is co-ordinating the range of other people the child might need to see. For most children not in care, it is their parents. For children in care, co-ordination falls between different people and there is not the same clear, strong link between child and "parental" adult.

3.9 It is only the social worker and carer, and their teachers for those of school age, whom all children in care will see as part of their everyday lives. Beyond this, there are very few professionals whom children in care see *because* they are in care rather than because of a need which any child might have. However, the fact that children in care often have more complex needs mean they will often see more people, making a lack of consistency in the person co-ordinating these contacts especially damaging.

3.10 The proposals set out in this Green Paper will mean that, while like any other children they will come into contact with a range of adults in their lives, for the vast majority of children in care there will be just three key individuals who between them exercise the parental advocacy role:

- Social worker;

- Carer (whether in residential or foster care); and

- Independent advocate (see below)

3.11 For children with complex needs arising out of a disability, the role of lead professional is particularly crucial. Their role includes ensuring that disabled children's health needs are fully met, particularly where they require a specialist service; and that full pre-placement and on-going plans are put in place and reflect the communication needs of children with impaired communications.

A consistent parenting role

3.12 The reality is that because placements do – and sometimes should – change, the social worker is generally the best person to take on this consistent parental role. In this chapter our focus is on how the social worker as representative of the corporate parent can become a more consistent figure and more effective at co-ordinating services.

3.13 There are, however, real practical problems with this. Many children in care experience frequent changes of social worker, and we know that there is a turnover rate of 11%[22] in children's social work.

" You get to know one then they leave."

---

22 Expressed as the number of leavers from social services departments in the 12 months to 30 September 2005 as a percentage of the total number employed

Options for Excellence

3.14 Addressing problems in recruitment and retention of social workers is at the heart of the Options for Excellence Review, the final report of which will be published shortly. Social workers have a range of responsibilities to children in care and should respond to them as individuals. There are particular issues for some children, such as the need for a placement with good access for children with disabilities or the need to refer children to education colleagues in order to consider whether it is necessary to carry out a statutory assessment of special educational needs. The children we spoke to in preparing this Green Paper were very clear that this role can only be carried out successfully if social workers are sensitive and responsive to such issues.

3.15 The Options for Excellence report will contain short and longer term options, which we will consider as part of the Comprehensive Spending Review process, to improve recruitment, retention and quality of practice for all social workers and the wider social care workforce by:

- Developing mechanisms to help employers remodel their workforce with new roles and flexible ways of working;

- Proposing a 'Newly Qualified Social Worker' status to define and support the training, supervision and mentoring requirements of new social workers;

- Strengthening Continuing Professional Development across the workforce, making better use of research and developing an employer endorsed charter for CPD;

- Supporting skills for social workers as commissioners with a qualifications framework to improve commissioning practice; and

- Introducing measures to improve the use of technology across the social care sector such as access to equipment, skills and training.

Social care practices

3.16 Children's social workers are in no doubt that their job is to help children. They have told us that they are frustrated with a complex system that takes them away from direct work with children. They also have only limited freedom to act as a vocal and effective advocate for the child, ensuring they receive the support they need. In our most recent survey, over half of local authorities reported problems with both recruitment and retention because of the nature of the work.

3.17 This is a long-standing problem and addressing it needs real reform. There must be much greater scope for independence and innovation for social workers. Social workers want to be able to spend more time working with children and their families, but often find this difficult because of high caseloads and the need to respond to crisis situations. Clearly, child protection must be the first priority, but social workers also need the freedom to work with children on a sustained basis to improve their long term outcomes. We need to shift the culture, draw clear lines of accountability and improve working conditions to free social workers to do this. They should be able to build strong and lasting relationships with children and their families, and act as a strong advocate for the child's interests.

3.18 Some local authorities have taken great steps towards this by organising themselves into specialised teams with a strong focus on delivering the lead professional role for children.

3.19 We want to go much further than this. We believe there can be an inherent tension for social workers operating within the local authority. On the one hand they must do what is best for children but on the other must defend the authority's existing policies and practices and work within its structures. And the many levels of management within authorities can mean that decisions about children are taken by people who have no direct knowledge of that child and their needs.

3.20 To address this we propose to:

- **Explore a model of 'social care practices': small groups of social workers undertaking work with children in care commissioned by but independent of local authorities**

3.21 A practice would be an autonomous organisation, whether a voluntary or community sector organisation, a social enterprise or a private business – similar to a GP practice – registered with the Commission for Social Care Inspection and responsible for employing social workers. This would be a tremendous opportunity for social workers and for children.

3.22 Working in a practice commissioned by local authorities, each social worker would have the freedom to concentrate on the children in their care and would be accountable for their outcomes. While the local authority would still be responsible for care proceedings, once the child entered care formally they would be given a lead professional from a practice, charged with the task of being a consistent parental figure and advocate for the child. That lead professional would remain with them, as far as possible, throughout their time in care and beyond to support successful returns home.

3.23 Each practice would hold a budget, provided through the contract with the authority, and would use it for individual social workers to fund the placement, support and activities that they believe 'their' children should have. Social workers would be given the autonomy and the freedom from a complex management structure needed to be able to put the child above everything else.

3.24 The members of the practice would play a strong parental role in all the key aspects of a child's life. They would take a strong interest in the child's education, including helping the child and their carers make decisions about the best school for the child and acting as a parental advocate to get the best from the school and to address specific issues such as possible exclusions.

3.25 They would have a genuine financial and personal stake in a small organisation centred around them and the children in their care. The opportunities are immense. Practices would be able to develop multi-disciplinary teams including staff such as education welfare officers as well as social workers to develop a unique offer in response to particular needs.

3.26 By developing their own style and approach, different practices might appeal to different children. Some might offer a greater focus on long term care for children with complex needs, for example, children with serious disabilities, while others could focus their efforts on work with families to address parental problems and help children return home successfully. As different styles evolve, it will be increasingly possible to offer authorities, children and families a choice of which practice is best able to meet their needs.

3.27 Successful practices would be able to expand and grow and to invest in better support services through a model of performance contracting. Under this approach, agencies are offered a powerful incentive to achieve permanence for children through being paid a set amount per child. They would be free to retain unused funds – either as profit or for reinvestment, depending on the nature of the organisation – resulting from a successfully managed and supported return home, or to adoption.

3.28 Local authorities would continue to play a key role. They would make the assessments and determine the budget for each practice. As part of the contract process they would monitor the quality of the care being provided.

3.29 This represents radical change and while we believe strongly that this is the right direction there are many issues to consider. Therefore we will:

- **Establish a working group, to report in Spring 2007, to explore the feasibility of piloting social care practices including how to set in place a robust system of performance management.**

Budget-holding for lead professionals

3.30 Children have told us that their social worker often does not have the power to take decisions on their behalf, frequently having to refer back to their superiors within the local authority rather than being able to respond directly to the child's request.

3.31 For social workers to be truly able to respond to children's needs they must have the greatest freedom possible over what support the child gets and when. The proposals set out above on social care practices provide one way of offering this kind of freedom, and the working group will test out the model in detail.

3.32 However, it is unlikely that such a model would become commonplace across the country quickly, and it is therefore important also to explore ways of freeing social workers to provide better services for children within a local authority. Having a budget can make a big difference to this.

The model of performance contracting used in **Illinois** includes expectations about outcomes in standard contracts. Each year, providers are paid a set amount and required to bring a set number of children into their care. Those who are successful at resettling these children back with their families, or into adoption, will have lower costs as a result, and will effectively be able to realise more of the fee they have been paid as profit. Since the introduction of performance contracting, permanency in Illinois has increased by around 150% and stability by 20%.

Tendayi's social worker was given a bursary by the local authority to support her education in the run-up to her GCSEs, in which the school had predicted that she would get mainly E and G grades. The bursary was used to provide additional tuition in English, food technology and health and social care. Some of the money was also used to provide Tendayi with a set of books to help her revise.

Over the course of ten weeks Tendayi received weekly tuition in each subject and was able to complete her coursework and feel more confident about taking the final exams. Tendayi achieved higher than expected grades in health and social care and English, and enrolled on a college course in September.

There is a world of difference between being able to place a request for funding when a child asks for money to buy new sports equipment and being able to produce the money there and then.

3.33 We believe that social workers, with carers, are the best people to judge what the children they care for need and should be given the flexibility to respond quickly. Research[23] demonstrates that models where professionals are given autonomy over a ring-fenced budget allocated to a particular child can provide improved quality of life for service users and their families. The clarity which fund-holding brings to the use of resources can help to ensure both creativity in developing service packages and an efficient mix with informal care.

3.34 We are already piloting this budget-holding lead professional model, and these experiments are beginning to show that the approach works for vulnerable children in other areas. We will:

- **Pilot budget-holding by the lead professional for children in care, their social worker, to see how effective the role can be for children in care.**

3.35 These pilots will test out the impact of differing amounts of money – all of which will give the lead professional significant purchasing power and leverage – and provide a maximum flexibility to put together packages of individualised support across a wide range of areas. This approach would offer social workers far greater freedom in how they address the needs of children, and to agree with children themselves how the budget should be spent. The wide range of relevant services could include:

- Therapeutic interventions such as speech or language therapy, or emotional support from appropriately qualified practitioners;
- Sporting and leisure activities;
- Travel costs;
- Parenting support groups and other work with birth families;
- School holiday activities;
- Childcare/play schemes;
- Youth activities/workshops; and
- Significant one-off payments.

3.36 The pilots will explore the level of budget which could be held by social workers and we will encourage local authorities to be as

---

23 Office for Public Management, on behalf of DfES (2006): *Budget-Holding Lead Professionals – literature review*

Trafford are currently piloting a fund-holding lead professional model for children with additional complex needs. The lead professional can spend up to £200 per child in any one week, drawn from a budget pooled by local partners including the PCT, Connexions, and the Youth Offending Team. Lead Professionals are able to discuss and agree the support needed with child and the family, and then go out and buy it.

innovative as possible. We will work with one of the pilot areas to consider if the budget could include funding for the cost of the child's placement.

3.37 Both budget-holding and social care practices, which will give social workers greater flexibility to obtain services from a wider range of providers, are likely to be of particular benefit to disabled children and young people.

3.38 The social worker's budget will be in addition to funds held by them to help secure personalised support for children in care in schools, which we consider in chapter 5.

The care plan

3.39 Irrespective of the way in which social workers operate in organisational terms, it is important that care is planned effectively around all of the child's needs. Every child in care is required to have a care plan setting out the type of care and support they receive. This plan should be a 'living document', considered at the child's regular review meetings. It must reflect the needs, circumstances and background of the child ensuring, for example, that their cultural and religious beliefs are respected and supported by those working with them.

3.40 The vast majority of children in care already have such a plan but our conversations

with them show that many do not know it exists or what it contains.

" It's supposed to be changed every 6 months but mine says it's 2001 and says I'm 9.*"*

" I don't know. What is a care plan?*"*

3.41 It is vital, especially for the many children who change placements or social workers, that there is a care plan which addresses all aspects of their lives and which children have been genuinely involved in drawing up. It is the task of Independent Reviewing Officers, discussed in more detail in chapter 8, to ensure that this is done appropriately. We will:

● **Issue revised guidance to all local authorities on the creation, management and use of children's care plans and what their contents should be, including setting out the positive activities in which young people have chosen to take part. The guidance will set out who will access children's care plans, and when, through the Integrated Children's System.**

3.42 The care plan should be a tool in helping children set a pathway through life and should reflect their personal ambitions. For some, the plan will be focused on helping prepare the child and their family for a return home. For others, especially older children, it should focus on longer term goals and how they will be achieved. We will:

- **Require that care plans for all children in care must set out long term ambitions, agreed with the children (if they are of a suitable age and level of understanding), and what will be done whilst in care to help the child achieve them.**

Independent Advocates

3.43 Our discussions with children in care have shown that there is often an adult who has played a crucial role in the child's life, encouraging them to succeed and advocating for them when required. This will be a different person for different children – for example, it might be a teacher from their school. But not everyone is lucky enough to develop this relationship spontaneously and we believe that every child in care must be offered a mentor who is independent of the system, able to befriend them and support them when they need it.

3.44 The Children Act 1989 introduced a requirement on local authorities to recruit an Independent Visitor for every child who had little or no contact with their birth family. The Independent Visitor would befriend the child and give them someone outside the care system to talk to about how things are going.

3.45 We believe this role has huge potential for all children in care, not just those who are no longer in touch with their family. It could provide children with an independent source of encouragement, advice and support – and, if the child wants it, advocacy. Independent visitors are not child care professionals: they are interested, committed volunteers. And children who currently have independent visitors have told us that it is very important to them that their visitor is a volunteer: someone who chooses to spend time with them rather than a paid professional.

" It's nice to have another friend to go out with. It's nice to have someone there when you need to talk."

3.46 While some good practice exists, not all local authorities provide Independent Visitors for those children in care who are currently eligible and who want this kind of mentor. We want to use this Green Paper to revitalise and rename the scheme, requiring all local authorities to meet their obligations in this area, and to consult on whether the

Natalie, aged 15, had lived in a residential unit for five years and had no contact with her family. Because of her autism and some challenging behaviour, the possibility of moving to a family placement had been discounted by her social worker. However, her Independent Visitor, Christine, started inviting Natalie to her home for tea once a fortnight. Natalie enjoyed mixing with Christine's three children and had not displayed any difficult behaviour after six months. With Natalie's agreement, Christine discussed this with her social worker. As a result, social services started looking into the possibility of finding a family placement for Natalie. Christine was able to contribute a lot of useful information to the planning meetings, including a written report of Natalie's visits to her home, so that the planning of her future could be carried out as carefully as possible.

offer of an Independent Visitor should be extended to other children in care. The scheme would be renamed to Independent Advocate to send a clear signal about how they could offer the child someone who was truly independent of the "system" and who could act as their advocate.

3.47 We do not believe that it would be appropriate for every child in care to be offered an Independent Advocate – for example, it would not be appropriate for children who spend a very short time in care. We will consider which children should be offered an Independent Advocate during the consultation period.

3.48 Nor do we believe that it would be helpful to dictate that the Independent Advocate must advocate for the young person or that they must be involved in a particular way – for example, by attending the care review meetings. The relationship will be different for different children and it should be for the young person to decide how involved they would like their Independent Advocate to be. For example, children in care who make a formal complaint to the local authority are already entitled to advocacy services for the duration of that complaint and they may or may not want their new Independent Advocate to become involved.

3.49 Following an announcement in this year's Pre-Budget Report, we are establishing a pilot programme, worth £1.5m from now until March 2008, to be delivered mainly through voluntary and community organisations, to examine mentoring for looked after children aged between 10-15. Organisations will be invited to submit proposals to the Department for Education

and Skills shortly and the outcomes from these pilots would inform our plans for implementing a new Independent Advocate scheme.

3.50 We therefore want to use this Green Paper to consult on:

- **Whether to revitalise the existing Independent Visitor scheme in order to introduce advocacy as a key element of the role and rename the scheme as "Independent Advocates"; and**

- **How best to offer an Independent Advocate to a wider group of children in care than those out of touch with their birth families.**

Questions for consultation

Do the proposals in this chapter add up to a sufficient strengthening of the corporate parenting role? If not what more should be done?

Would a 'social care practice' model help give social workers more freedom to support children?

Should the Independent Visitor role be revitalised and renamed as Independent Advocate to introduce advocacy as a key element of the role?

Chapter 4
Ensuring children are in the right placements

Summary

A happy, stable home life is fundamental to the successful development of all children and for children in care a successful placement is the most important factor in enabling them to flourish. Unfortunately, not all children are in placements which meet their needs and many are moved between placements far too frequently. We need radically to improve children's experience of placements, responding directly to what children themselves have told us is important and putting their views at the heart of placement decisions. Our proposals include:

- Piloting new regional commissioning units with interested local authorities to secure better value for money and make sure children are offered a choice of placements;

- Developing new Multi-Dimensional Treatment Foster Care pilots to test the effectiveness of this model with much younger children as well as adolescents;

- Developing a national 'tiered' model of placement types underpinned by a national qualifications framework for foster and residential carers;

- Investing in a locally delivered campaign to recruit foster carers from a diverse range of backgrounds;

- Including specialised professional development modules on working with vulnerable groups such as disabled young people and Unaccompanied Asylum Seeking Children within the proposed national training framework;

- Revising the assessment processes and support for family and friends carers to recognise that most will only ever care for one child; and

- Introducing a new 'special measures' regime to ensure swift action where standards are not met in children's homes.

4.1 We know that positive parenting has a significant effect on educational attainment[24]. The school a child attends is of course critical to their ability to succeed in education but more important still is the home environment. If we are to meet the

---

24 *The impact of parental involvement, parental support and family education on pupil attainment* (2003), Deforges,

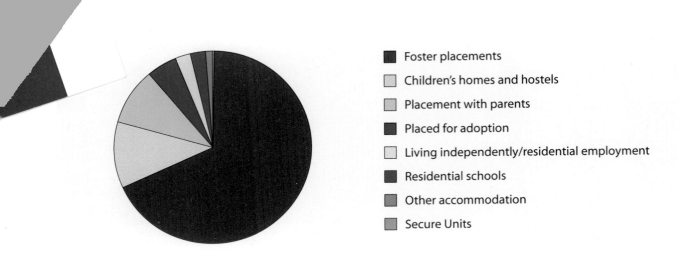

Foster placements

Children's homes and hostels

Placement with parents

Placed for adoption

Living independently/residential employment

Residential schools

Other accommodation

Secure Units

educational ambitions set out in this Green Paper it is vital that each child is in a placement which meets his or her individual needs.

4.2 Children and young people in care are placed in a variety of settings, from placements at home with their birth parents to small specialist residential care units. The large majority, though, are in foster care, and a minority live in residential care placements, hostels or residential schools.[25]

4.3 For many children care is a positive time in their lives, following their rescue from damaging home environments and giving them the opportunity to thrive. Both foster carers and residential care workers devote

huge energy and commitment to the children in their care and where they work well, placements meet children's needs extremely well, enabling attachments to develop which can build resilience and help sustain children through life's difficulties.

4.4 In a recent report from the Children's Rights Director, over half of the children in care who were asked said that their present placement was definitely the right one for them.[26] However, sadly this is not the case for all children in care. Far too many find themselves in placements which do not meet their needs, resulting in a high level of instability.

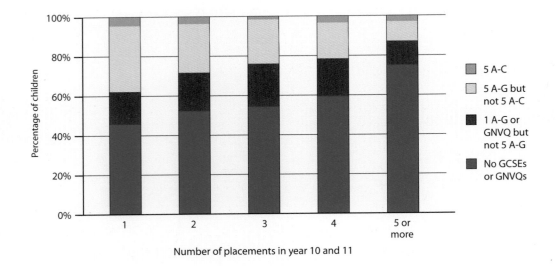

25 *Children looked after by Local Authorities Year Ending 31 March 05*, Volume 1: National Tables, National Statistics/Department for Education and Skills

26 *Placements, Decisions and Reviews: A Children's Views Report*, Children's Rights Director (2006)

4.5 Around 1 in 10 of the children who ceased to be in care in 2005 had 9 or more placements while in care, and only 65% of children who had been in care for over 21/2 years had been in the same placement for two years or more. The impact this has on children is marked as the graph above shows.

The impact of our reforms

4.6 In addressing the problems set out above, this Green Paper builds on a solid foundation of improvement. Government initiatives such as Quality Protects, the Care Standards Act 2000 and the DfES PSA target on placement stability for children in care have all contributed to a reduction in severe instability, with a fall in the percentage of children in care having three or more placement changes in any single year from 16% to 13% since 1998.

4.7 We have also placed a far stronger emphasis on the value of adoption as a positive option for children unable to return to their birth families. Reforms to the adoption system through the Adoption and Children Act 2002 ensured more support for families and required local authorities to place the child at the centre of decision-making. Adoption and Special Guardianship Orders are important ways of providing permanence for children in care, and the numbers benefiting have grown significantly with adoptions rising by 38% between 2000 and 2005.

4.8 Fundamental to the impact of these reforms has been the innovative approaches taken at local level, where investment and creativity on the ground have delivered real change.

Improving commissioning

4.9 It is vital that every child is given a choice of placements which meet their needs, create a good learning environment and offer value for money. Local authorities are responsible for commissioning all placements for children in care. There is currently a mixed economy of provision – for example, around 62% of children's homes are run by the private sector, 32% by local authorities, and 6% by voluntary sector providers.

4.10 Children in care have told us that having a choice over where they live is very important. It is also important to them that they know in advance some details about the placement. For example, if they are moving to a new foster placement, children want to know things such as whether there are other children in the placement, what religion the family has or whether their foster family has pets or a back garden. Children with physical disabilities told us that the size and layout of a placement is particularly important for them. We want all local authorities to offer children in care a choice of placements, and comprehensive details about the placements in advance, in order that they can be more meaningfully involved in deciding where they will live.

4.11 We believe that the proposals in this Green Paper to improve the recruitment and status of foster carers, alongside the increasing expertise in local authorities to manage the local market of placements, will enable more and more local authorities to offer such a choice.

4.12 We know also that a lack of effective planning and market management can lead to children being placed outside their home authority. Nearly a third of children in care are in placements outside the local authority area which cares for them. For some children, being placed away from their home area is a sensible and child-centred choice. For example, children with very complex needs may need specialist therapeutic residential provision which is delivered very effectively by a number of voluntary sector organisations. But this may simply not be available locally. Where a child is placed far from home for these reasons, we expect local authorities to ensure they are in close touch with the child and those caring for them, monitoring the placement closely. But most children in care want to remain in the area which is most familiar to them.

"If you're put into care you should be able to stay in the town or part of the county you came from so you can stay with your mates."

4.13 Children placed far away from their home are less likely to succeed in education (though in some cases this will reflect the more complex needs of the child rather than being solely a consequence of the distance from home). 55% of children placed out of authority fail to achieve any GCSEs compared to 48% of those in their local authority[27].

4.14 The need to improve commissioning is illustrated further by rising placement costs. Local authorities currently spend about £1.9 billion per year on children's placements compared to £1.3 billion in 2000/01 and the evidence is that value for money is not being achieved, with no statistical link between unit costs and educational outcomes.

4.15 Nearly half of the overall expenditure on placements relates to the 13% of children placed in residential care. Placement costs vary significantly between different local authorities and this cannot all be explained by differences in the type of provision or socio-economic differences between regions.

4.16 This is reinforced by recently published research[28] which found that, on the whole, too high a price is being paid for placements involving a range of levels of support. Underlying causes for this include a lack of transparency in costs, a shortage of experienced managers able to manage local markets successfully, and limited dialogue between suppliers and commissioners. Commissioning problems are particularly acute in relation to very challenging children. Clearly, commissioning strategies must also reflect local need and it is vital that they are reflected in the local Children and Young People's Plan, which will have been drawn together following detailed consultation with local communities.

4.17 In order to disseminate the lessons from this research and to improve commissioning across the board, we will:

- **Publish guidance in 2007 for managing local placement markets; and**

---

27 The local authority of placement is unknown for 44% of care-leavers in 2004-05. This was collected for children in foster care and residential care only.

28 PriceWaterhouseCoopers (2006) *DfES Children's Services: Children's Homes and Fostering*

Local authorities in the **West Midlands** are developing a regional resource to support local authority commissioning strategies. The unit will provide strategic and planning capacity to the fourteen local authorities in the region. The aim of the unit will be to achieve better co-ordination of commissioning arrangements, providing a central source of information, knowledge and advice.

Local authorities in the **North East** have established a Regional Commissioning Unit, supported by the Regional Partnership and Government Office North East. The joint funded Unit is working closely with LAs, Primary Care Trusts, the Strategic Health Authority and other partners to co-ordinate information, evaluate provision and make recommendations to regional agencies on value for money, new service arrangements and high quality outcomes for the placement of children with complex needs.

- **Work with individual local authorities who are experiencing difficulties with commissioning to improve their practice and the value for money they secure.**

4.18 Much work has already been done by and with local authorities to improve commissioning, including the development of better regional approaches to commissioning and contracting through the Choice Protects initiative and the Regional Partnerships, leading to local level improvements in commissioning.

4.19 However, the evidence of practical difficulties across the country suggests that more is needed to help improve commissioning in a way which does not place additional burdens on local authorities but which spreads the lessons from research and good practice more widely. In order to enable local authorities to combine their purchasing power, thereby exercising greater leverage over the placement market, we will:

- **Pilot, with interested local authorities and existing partnerships, new regional commissioning units.**

4.20 These units will build on existing models of excellent practice developed here and elsewhere such as the work of Regional Centres of Excellence and performance contracting. As discussed in chapter 3, under that model providers are funded in a way which offers greater rewards for securing better outcomes for the children in their care. The units will:

- Undertake commissioning on behalf of local authorities, drawing on the support of the Regional Centres of Excellence, Government Offices, other regional organisations and the NHS where appropriate;

- Model the needs of the local and regional population and forecast placement requirements accordingly;

- Respond to assessments of need by social workers in offering individuals a choice of placements;

- Improve market management by making effective use of block contracting and other approaches to get a good mix of local authority, private and voluntary sector provision;

- Develop supplier development strategies to maximise providers' competitiveness and quality of service;

- Develop a deep understanding of local market conditions and trends; and

- Pass savings back to local authorities to re-invest in front line services.

4.21 We would also require the units to:

- **Offer a choice of suitable placements for each child, leaving final decisions about individual placements in the hands of social workers in discussion with children themselves.**

Increasing the choice of placements

22 Children have also told us that they are rarely given any say about the type of placement to which they are allocated, despite the existing statutory duty to consult them and give due consideration to their views. There is some good practice in this area but many children report having decisions made for them with little or no consultation. Social workers themselves may have little choice in the placements they can obtain and as a result can do little to pass on real choice to the child.

" I said I wanted to move and you have to say it for them to hear."

4.23 For a group with needs as diverse and complicated as children in care a wide range of placements, with real choice for the child, is absolutely critical. We know

that children enter care with very different levels and type of need. They often enter care for very different reasons, and their lengths of stay in care vary substantially.

4.24 While some authorities have explicitly structured their placements in order to mirror this complexity, in many areas the split tends to be less complex and there is evidence that children are not being offered placements which match their needs. Only 52% of local authority fostering services and 60% of independent fostering agencies meet the 'matching' standards[29]. In order to address this problem it is vital that social workers are able to access a choice of appropriate placements each time a move is required.

4.25 A residential setting will best meet the needs of some children but for the majority of children in care a placement in a family environment will be most suitable. It is worrying that local authorities across the country report a shortage in foster placements within both their own provision and what is available from independent providers. The Fostering Network estimates that the shortage stands at as many as 8,000 placements across England.

4.26 We know that the type of placement which a child is in affects his or her educational performance significantly. The educational outcomes of children whose last placement is in residential care are even worse than those of other children, with 73% failing to get even a single GCSE. This is in part because children in residential

---

29 Part of the framework of National Minimum Standards. The matching standard is an assessment of whether the carer children are placed with is capable of meeting his or her assessed needs.

In **Denmark** those working with children in nurseries and pre-schools, as well as care settings, undertake a three and a half year degree level qualification. The majority of care is undertaken in residential settings, though there are a vast range of options including a high level of support in families and children are encouraged to see care as a home.

France has a number of types of *éducateurs*, trained to work with children, young people and adults with additional needs, including children in residential care, and a specialist role supporting children in foster care. *Éducateurs* receive three years' full time training or 4-5 years in-service training and are required to have three years of relevant work experience.

Germany has a range of placement types, centred around residential care but ranging from full-time care to outreach to support placements in families. There are distinct levels of training for those working with children, ranging from a three year vocational qualification, through a four year degree course and higher degrees leading to managerial or supervisory positions.

care tend to have more complex needs than those in family settings, but the difference is striking.

4.27 We know that there is a shortage of skills and qualifications in both foster and residential care. Only 5% of foster carers have an NVQ3 qualification relevant to working with children and social workers frequently report that although the quality of care may be excellent, support for schooling and education is often lacking. In residential care over 40% of managers lack a relevant qualification for working with children and only 5% of children's homes can demonstrate that at least 80% of their staff have a relevant NVQ3 or equivalent qualification[30].

4.28 In considering the type of placements which should be available for children in care, there is much to learn from other countries. Other countries have very different models of care from ours, including approaches in which carers are highly skilled and are recognised as expert professionals. Many are experts in "social

pedagogy", an approach which looks at the child in a holistic way, focusing on their development. Social pedagogy is grounded in a broad theoretical base spanning education, health and psychology and includes a wide range of skills including creative and practical subjects.

4.29 These systems all have in common a framework for matching levels of intensity of support with the levels of need amongst the populations they serve. Some parts of the UK are already developing different types and levels of care in this way, for example Multi-Dimensional Treatment Foster Care (see box overleaf) and the results in terms of improved placement stability are already evident.

4.30 We want all local authorities to develop a range of types and levels of placement and we propose to:

---

30 The State of Social Care in England 2004-05, Commission for Social Care Inspection (2005)

In the **Multi-Dimensional Treatment Foster Care England** (MTFCE) project for 10-16 year olds, which we are currently piloting in 19 areas across the UK, foster carers complete their local authority's "Skills to Foster" training, undergo a process of formal assessment and approval and are then given an extra three days' MTFCE training. The scheme follows a model developed by the University of Oregon which has been shown to be an effective alternative to residential provision. The model includes teams providing intensive support to foster carers, children and birth families. Teams include programme supervisors and managers, birth-family therapists, foster-care recruiters and supporters, individual therapists, skills trainers and educational staff.

The programme has achieved a substantial increase in placement stability: whereas some of the young people had moved up to 15 times in the previous year, only 7 of 33 had left MTFCE after less than 3 months in the programme.

- **Develop new Multi-Dimensional Treatment Foster Care pilots to test the effectiveness of this model with much younger children as well as adolescents; and**

- **Consult on developing a national 'tiered' model of placement types underpinned by a national qualifications framework for foster and residential carers.**

4.31 This tiered model would be structured around the needs of children, with carers being trained and skilled to a greater or lesser degree depending on children's individual requirements. The model would offer a ladder of career progression for carers who would have the option of developing their skills to enter higher tiers.

4.32 The framework would offer a competency based approach available to all foster carers and staff and managers in residential homes as well as other professionals such as social workers and designated teachers. The structure of competencies and qualifications offered, and summarised below, would incorporate the principles of social pedagogy. Through this framework professionals working with children in care would be able to develop a common language and approach based around a core understanding of children's development.

" When they are new staff I get asked if it is ok to for them to do my personal care and I feel I can't say no when really I would like to get to know them first.*"*

4.33 Professionals would be much better equipped to respond to the individual needs of the child. The framework would include information on understanding how a range of issues, including culture, religion, disability and sexuality, can affect children and young people. This will ensure that the carers supporting children in care are sensitive to these issues and informed about how to support the needs of individual children.

4.34 The model would be underpinned by:

- A new framework of skills and qualifications incorporating the principles of social pedagogy to support the tiered approach, set out in national occupational standards;

TIER 1 – CHILDREN WITH FEW ADDITIONAL NEEDS RELATIVE TO THOSE OUTSIDE CARE

Carers' competencies: Child development, attachment, separation and loss; health and wellbeing; communication with children, and involving them in decisions; risk and protective factors associated with resilience; the importance of school and learning; parenting techniques and managing behaviour; supporting contact; supporting access to and participation in cultural and sporting activities; working with children of different ethnicities, faiths, cultures, and sexualities; and techniques for teaching basic life skills

Support for carers: Support groups with other carers; opportunities to train with other carers; and guidance on accessing parenting services and universal provision.

TIER 2 – CHILDREN WITH SOME ADDITIONAL NEEDS

Carers' competencies: Knowledge of techniques for working with children with more complex needs, e.g. parenting techniques, Treatment Foster Care, work with disabled children, working with unaccompanied asylum seeking children (UASC), and dealing with substance misuse.

Support for carers: Records held by authorities of skills, competencies, and "style" of carers; monitoring of placements and behaviour of children; the possibility to take on additional paid work, e.g. outreach with children living with birth families.

TIER 3 – CHILDREN WITH SEVERE OR COMPLEX NEEDS REQUIRING SPECIALIST CARE

Carers' competencies: Delivering an intensive, structured support programme with the social worker and other agencies; expertise in techniques for supporting vulnerable children; support, guidance and training to other foster/residential carers.

Support for carers: Weekly, or even daily, reporting of problem behaviours; support groups with other tier 3 carers; a specific plan for the use of short breaks; a multi-disciplinary team around the child and placement to meet specific needs.

- A new Foundation Degree in working with children in care to ensure that care is seen as a key part of the children's workforce. Successful students would attain the status of "children in care expert practitioner" which would be available also to other professionals including designated teachers;

- A degree-level qualification as an extension of this foundation degree for those wishing to build on it;

- Revised National Minimum Standards for fostering services and residential care linking explicitly to this new framework;

- A revised framework for fees building on the national minimum allowances for foster care and setting out the level of fees which might be associated with each tier;

- A mandatory national registration scheme for foster carers, putting them on a par with their colleagues in social work, residential care and other parts of the children's workforce.

Increasing the availability of foster placements

4.35 One of the aims of the tiered framework described above is to enable social workers to access a good foster care placement for every child whose needs would best be met in a family setting. Increasing the number of foster carers is therefore an essential part of the strategy. We have already funded a number of initiatives aimed at improving foster carer recruitment including £2m for a national recruitment campaign in 2000; a Fostering Publicity Pack in 2004; and funding to both the Fostering Network and local authorities to improve recruitment and retention.

4.36 Many local authorities and independent foster care providers have developed innovative and successful strategies to recruit and retain carers such as round-the-clock support and advice. However, as mentioned above the Fostering Network still estimates that there is a national shortage of around 8,000 foster carers.

4.37 We know that there are particular recruitment issues in London where children are almost twice as likely to be placed out of authority compared with other parts of the country. Over half of all children in care in London are from black or minority ethnic backgrounds, meaning that recruiting carers from a diverse range of backgrounds is especially important. We know that it can be important for children's sense of identify to be placed with carers from a similar cultural or ethnic background, and will offer guidance on successful approaches to doing this as part of our recruitment campaign.

4.38 Building on recent research and the success of local recruitment strategies, we will:

- **Invest in a locally delivered campaign to recruit foster carers from a diverse range of backgrounds, working with local authorities to build on the lessons we have learned from previous experience and from research.**

4.39 For some foster carers, the size of their home can limit the number of children they are able to look after. And we know that lack of space can also act as a disincentive to people thinking of becoming foster carers in the future.

4.40 The Homebuy equity sharing scheme offers one opportunity for addressing this issue. Homebuy offers social tenants, key workers and other priority first time buyers an opportunity to get on the housing ladder. Those eligible receive an equity loan to help them purchase a home suitable for their needs which they would otherwise be unable to afford. Alternatively, purchasers may buy a minimum 25% share in a newly built house, generally offered by a housing association, and pay rent on the remainder. Foster carers are one group potentially eligible for this scheme, and in determining their local priorities we would encourage every local authority to:

- **Consider whether foster carers should be included as a priority within the Homebuy scheme in their area.**

Improving the availability of other types of placement

4.41 While the majority of children in care are best placed with family or friends, in fostering or residential placements, a minority of children – often with the most severe needs – require more specialist placements. Young people with exceptionally challenging behaviour, and children with severe and complex health needs or disabilities may require placements tailored to their individual circumstances. Similarly, unaccompanied asylum seeking children may require specialist support and because of their special circumstances, may be subject to a different placement regime. As mentioned earlier in this paper, there is a separate Home Office reform.

4.42 It is vital that local authorities have access to more specialist types of placement within their commissioning strategies to make sure that these young people's needs are met. We therefore propose to:

- **Include specialised professional development modules on working with disabled young people within the national framework proposed above;**

- **Incorporate specialist professional development options on caring for UASC (e.g. knowledge of the asylum system) within the training framework proposed above; and**

- **Give lead workers for UASC within the Home Office's Immigration and Nationality Directorate access to the national training framework proposed in this chapter.**

4.43 Around 9% of children in care are placed with family or friends and there is evidence that this type of placement could be used

effectively for more children[31]. In order to encourage this type of placement, we will:

- **Explore whether assessment processes and support for family and friends care should be revised to recognise that most will only ever care for one child.**

4.44 Concurrent planning, in which children are placed with foster carers who are also approved as adopters, can also offer a smooth route to permanence for some children. We want to encourage greater use of this approach and will:

- **Explore ways of encouraging more use of concurrent planning, for instance through disseminating good practice and extending the right to leave from work, already provided to new adoptive parents, to concurrent carers.**

4.45 Together this package of proposals for increasing the range of available placements will yield increased choice for social workers seeking to make placements and reduce the need to rely on out-of-authority placements. In order to strengthen this we propose to:

- **Introduce a requirement that local authorities can place children out-of-authority only if no suitable placement exists.**

4.46 Some disabled children spend 52 weeks of the year in residential special schools, but are not legally looked after by a local authority. This means that they do not have the statutory rights and protection afforded by being in the care of a local authority. Some believe that they should have looked after status. However, others are concerned that

---

31 Farmer and Moyers (2005) *Children Placed with Family and Friends: Placement Patterns and Outcomes*

Earthsea House in Norfolk, run in partnership between Norfolk County Council and the charity Childhood First, provides residential care and education for up to eight children aged five to 12. Earthsea offers support to children with complex needs and a 'family home' feel including a quiet room for children to start their day and a family style discussion around the dinner table with staff and children at the end of it. The home also offers specialised educational provision which responds to these children's particular needs. Staff are highly trained, coming from a range of professional backgrounds such as psychology or psychiatric nursing, and all are required to complete a diploma in psychosocial care run by Childhood First and Middlesex University.

parents of these disabled children would not welcome this because they would not perceive their children to have the same type of needs as other children in care. We therefore want to consult on whether:

- **Local authorities should be required to consider – in consultation with parents – whether disabled children in residential placements should have looked after status.**

4.47 We are also examining the benefits of boarding school placements for children in care and our approach on this is set in Chapter 5.

Improving the quality of residential care

4.48 Despite some excellent provision, care standards in some residential homes are inadequate and need to be addressed as a matter of urgency. Only 25% of residential homes meet 90% or more of the national minimum standards for care homes and there is anecdotal evidence that the quality of support for education is sometimes weak in residential care settings. This, combined with reports of a culture of failing to encourage attendance at school, suggests a need for children's homes and placing authorities to be held to account more rigorously.

4.49 Residential care will always be the placement of first choice for some children and we know that some children say that they do not want to be in foster care. We need these children to be able to enjoy a genuinely excellent care experience, drawing on the best of what homes in this country and elsewhere do now.

4.50 We want to look in more detail at the most effective practice in residential care and at what the very best providers offer to make such care a positive experience for children. We will therefore :

- **Include analysis of the characteristics of excellent residential care within the remit of a working group on placement choice to report in Spring 2007.**

4.51 In order to rationalise and focus the current array of national standards governing residential care, we are undertaking a review of the National Minimum Standards (NMS) and associated regulations, set to finish in 2008.

4.52 We expect that the revised standards and associated regulations will offer a much clearer, more focused set of NMS. Following the introduction of the new NMS, we propose to:

- **Introduce a new 'special measures' regime to ensure swift action where standards are not met in children's homes.**

4.53 Following the introduction of that regime, any residential care provider failing to meet one or more of the NMS at an inspection would be placed in 'special measures' and required to produce an improvement plan within 28 days. Failure to deliver that plan within the time scale specified by the inspectorate would result in an absolute ban on any more children being placed there. Inspectors would also be able to require that those children already placed there will be removed in a planned way within a specified period.

4.54 If problems were not resolved within the specified period, the inspectorate would immediately begin procedures to de-register the failing home. As we made clear in our response to *Safeguarding Children: the second joint Chief Inspectors' Report on Arrangements to Safeguard Children*, we will:

- **Reintroduce a statutory duty for social workers to visit children placed in children's homes, with a greater frequency of visits for those placed out of authority.**

Questions for consultation

Should a tiered approach to fostering placements be developed? If so, should this be underpinned by a formal qualification framework?

How can we increase placement choice without increasing financial burdens on the system?

Should local authorities be required to consider whether disabled children in 52 week specialist residential provision should have "looked after" status?

Chapter 5
A first class education

Summary

A good education is the key to a positive future. We want every child to benefit from the opportunities which a good education can open up, from early years right through to further and higher education. Because of the trauma and other difficulties they bring with them, most children in care approach education at a disadvantage. It is therefore vital that schools and other educational settings recognise their particular needs and respond to them comprehensively, offering a high standard of education and support which enables them to catch up where necessary but also challenges them to reach their full potential. Our proposals include:

- Enabling carers to access early years support for children by developing specialised training, providing information about the free early education entitlement, and including support for children in care in the Early Years Foundation Stage guidance;

- Providing local authorities with the power to direct schools to admit children in care, even where the school is already fully subscribed through the Education and Inspections Bill currently before Parliament;

- Creating a presumption that children in care should not move schools in years 10-11, unless it is clearly in their best interests;

- Offering a free entitlement to school transport for children in care to allow them to remain in the same school after a placement move;

- Encouraging schools to offer an excellent personalised education to children in care, using the £990 million personalisation funding provided to schools for all children, supported by providing social workers with a personalised budget of around £500 per child per year to support children's education;

- Introducing a 'virtual head teacher' in every local authority, initially in a number of pilot authorities, to support schools in their work with children in care and build networks between schools and other education providers, carers and social workers;

- Introducing mandatory training on children in care for new Further Education College principals, as part of their qualification criteria; and

- Introducing a new pre-Apprenticeship programme to help young people gain the skills needed to start an Apprenticeship.

Percentage of children in care vs. all children attaining appropriate level by Key Stage (2004)

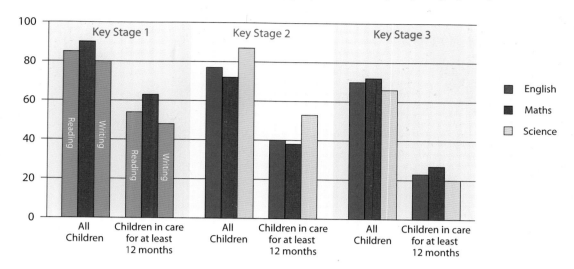

5.1 For many children in care, childhood is characterised by instability and uncertainty. As a result, their educational attainment is poor and they under-perform significantly compared to their peers at all stages of the education system. The attainment gap widens between Key stages 1 and 3 as the graph above shows:

5.2 We know that a lack of qualifications is strongly linked to poor outcomes in adult life. 60% of those not in education, employment or training at age 19 had no GCSEs on leaving care. Given the likelihood that in adult life children in care will have less support from their families than other young people, it is even more important that they are equipped with the right skills and qualifications for the future.

" I want to get a job and I need good grades."

5.3 Children in care have told us that education means a great deal to them. They want to do well at school and they understand that it makes a big difference to their future opportunities. But they believe they do not always get a fair deal in school because the links between school and the care system are not good enough. Our conversations with children showed that they do not feel schools always understand their needs and that sometimes being in care can result in them being singled out or bullied.

" My teacher said that 'social services called to see if you're playing truant'."

5.4 Some told us that they have been pulled out of lessons for meetings with carers or social workers, or have been made to feel awkward because they are in care. We need to find ways to give children better support in schools to help them realise their ambitions without making them feel stigmatised. Stronger relationships between schools, social workers and carers will be the key to achieving this goal.

Reform in schools and colleges

5.5 The proposals in this Green Paper are set against a background of ambitious reform in the education system as a whole. The White Paper *Higher Standards, Better Schools for All* set out our strategy for raising standards in all schools, ensuring that every child in every school in every community gets the education they need to enable them to fulfil their potential. These reforms will enable each school to develop its own distinctive ethos – whether they are specialist schools, Trust schools or Academies – so that they can drive their own development and improve the way they support every child.

5.6 In order to achieve this vision, we are reforming the curriculum and qualifications so that all young people are engaged by learning and pursuing opportunities which prepare them well for life. The *14-19 Implementation Plan* set out our vision that by 2013 85% of 19 year-olds should have achieved at least a Level 2 qualification, and that by 2015 90% of 17 year olds will be participating in some sort of education or training.

5.7 The introduction of Extended Schools provision is now offering children and their families greater opportunities to take part in positive activities outside normal school hours, and has the potential to really benefit foster carers and the children placed with them. The Directors of Children's Services now in every Local authority and directly accountable for the children in their area provide a real opportunity to ensure that all those reforms have a tangible impact on children in care.

Why is attainment so poor?

5.8 Many schools and colleges are excellent at identifying and addressing the needs of children in care, enabling them to fulfil their potential as individuals.

5.9 However, for a variety of reasons most children in care do not benefit from this kind of support:

- Few children in care access the full range of early years education provision;

- Many children in care move between care placements or educational settings too often. As a result, they spend significant amounts of time out of education and are far less likely to be in the best performing schools;

- Most children in care have high levels of need which, too often, are not recognised and addressed. Most schools have only a small number of children in care at any one time and may go long periods where they

The **Marlowe Academy** in Kent has a high proportion of children in care and offers them and all of its students a highly individual approach to learning. It replaced a school which had been in special measures until a term before it closed in 2005. The academy's new leadership team has focused on creating a positive ethos where students take individual responsibility for their learning and has made an encouraging start. GCSE results were double those of the predecessor school and students have settled to a school day which begins at 8.30 and ends at 5pm five days a week. All students have a daily individual study period in open learning bays, supported by learning mentors and from Year 9 onwards all have at least one vocational option. This allows flexibility for students particularly in Key Stage 4 to have a longer block of time to undertake more sustained work in their vocational options, for example in working on a performance in drama or dance or undertaking a 'curating' module in a local art gallery.

have none. As a result, schools often have little experience in providing the intensive support they need;

- Children in care do not have the benefit of an engaged parent ensuring a good education for their child, and too few care placements replicate this role effectively; and

- Too few children in care are encouraged or helped to progress in education and training post-16.

5.10 It is also important to remember that very few children are in care from the early years right through to post-16. We need an education system that is flexible enough to meet the needs of children in care at whatever point, and for however long, they are in care.

Early years education

5.11 The importance of quality early years provision to the healthy development of young children and to their readiness to learn once they reach school age is well known. Given the particular challenges they tend to have, children in care ought to benefit substantially from these services.

5.12 However, we are very concerned that children in care are currently failing to take advantage of the new entitlement to early years education. Evidence from local authorities suggests that they are even less likely to access their entitlement to free early years provision than children from families in the most deprived communities, despite being in the care of the local authority.

5.13 The reasons for this largely relate to lack of information. Foster carers and others responsible for children in care are very often not aware of their entitlements, and early years settings tend not to reach out proactively to these groups.

5.14 If we are to improve radically the ability of children in care to succeed in education, it is vital that we start early in the way that any good parent would. Local authorities now have a duty, under the Childcare Act 2006, to work with their partners in the health service and Jobcentre Plus to improve outcomes for all young children in their area and to reduce inequalities between them. As a result, in meeting this new duty, it will be vital that local authorities ensure that they are also encouraging children's centres to reach out to children in care and foster carers and ensure that they are accessing the support they are entitled to.

5.15 To help increase the take-up of early years services we propose to:

- **Develop training and support for foster carers on the benefits of early years education as part of the proposed Integrated Training Framework;**

- **Include material on supporting children in care in early years settings in the Early Years Foundation Stage guidance to be available to all early years providers in February 2007, for implementation in 2008; and**

- **Prioritise provision of information about the free early education entitlement to foster carers, encouraging carers to visit settings to choose the most appropriate setting for their child.**

Distribution of children in care while at school, by school performance quartile (2004)

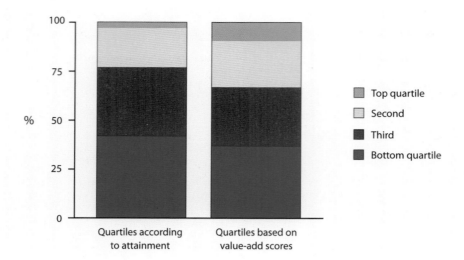

Being in a good school pre-16

5.16 Children in care are disproportionately less likely than their peers to be in high-performing schools.

5.17 And yet we know that children in care who attend schools in the top performance quartile make more progress than those placed in other schools.

5.18 Of course, we want every school to be a good school. The White Paper *Higher Standards, Better Schools for All* set out our plans for providing more resources and support to schools to enable them to offer a more personalised education for every child, with a new role for local authorities as the guarantor of high standards, intervening where provision is poor.

5.19 The White Paper also recognised the importance of harnessing the support and energy of parents. Every parent wants their child to receive the best possible education at a school that meets their particular needs and aptitudes. Our reforms are designed to place parents at the heart of education – with better access to regular information and more influence over the local system of schools.

5.20 Too often, children in care have missed out on the benefits of having engaged and committed parents. We need to ensure that, as corporate parent, the local authority places children in care in the most suitable school in the area.

5.21 Children in care already have the top priority in the normal admissions round. But this does not help when a child moves to a new placement during the school year when the only places available may be in weak, undersubscribed schools. We will in future ensure that local authorities as corporate parents have an effective choice in selecting schools for children in their care at any time.

● **From January 2007, subject to Parliamentary approval, local authorities will have the power to direct schools to admit children in care, even where the school is already fully subscribed.**

5.22 For the first time, the corporate parent will be able to ensure that where children in care move school it will be to the one which will best meet their needs – even if it is among the most popular and successful schools in their local area. This is a major change, and we need to ensure that the corporate parent navigates the system effectively. We therefore propose to:

- **Encourage local authorities to place children in care in the top performing schools in their area whenever they need to move school; and**

- **Undertake, as part of the new two-yearly reports on fair admissions, a review of the location of children in care in schools. This will demonstrate whether the new power for local authorities to place children in care in any school in the area is being used to best effect.**

5.23 As part of our reforms set out in *Higher Standards, Better Schools for All* we are introducing a new Choice Advice service, offering targeted support for those parents who may find it difficult to access information to assist them in applying for local schools on behalf of their child. This service will be available to social workers and foster carers as corporate parents, underpinning the admissions power set out above and helping them to choose the best school for each child in care.

5.24 As with other children, the mainstream education system is the best choice for most children in care. However, for some children in care, other educational settings will be more appropriate and it is vital that our proposals apply equally to the range of educational settings in which children in care may be placed.

Boarding Schools

5.25 For some children, boarding school could provide an excellent means of stability and support and some local authorities already use boarding school or other residential schools for their children in care.

5.26 Boarding schools can provide the right support and stability for some children in care, allowing them to take advantage of the strong ethos and emphasis on personal and social development which is characteristic of boarding provision. Boarding schools can also provide excellent access to support outside the classroom and a wide range of sporting and other activities which we know are crucial to positive outcomes. Of course boarding schools will not be right for all children in care, but for the minority whose carefully assessed individual needs indicate that such provision would be beneficial we want to see much better access and availability.

5.27 We are developing pilots in order to test the effectiveness of boarding provision for vulnerable children. The pilots will include 9 local authorities and around 50 independent and state maintained boarding schools and will begin in November 2006, running for 2 years. Through this Green Paper we will:

King Edward's School in Witley is a co-educational, independent boarding school in Surrey with a long history of educating children in care alongside young people from more stable backgrounds. The school is currently educating 5 children in care, who were placed there because their local authorities believed they would respond positively to the wide range of sporting, cultural and academic activity at the school, along with the strong emphasis on pastoral care.

- **Consult on whether the use of boarding provision for children in care could usefully be expanded, subject to the results of the evaluation of existing provision and pilots.**

Staying in a good school

5.28 Chapter 4 set out the data on placement moves, showing that the more placements a child has the less likely they are to succeed in education.

5.29 But it is not just placement moves which are disruptive to education. Children in care are also more likely than other children to move between educational settings more than once, and to join schools outside the normal admissions round, either because of changes in care placement or, in too many cases, exclusion. For example, around 1 in 5 of children in care join a new school in years 7-9 outside the normal admissions round compared with just 6% of all children. And around 15% of children in care join after September in years 10-11 compared with only 3% of all children[32]. We know that moving schools in year 11 has an immense negative impact on GCSE attainment.

5.30 Even when they secure a good school place children in care often miss a significant amount of school time. In 2005, one in eight children in care missed 25 or more days of school. Some authorities have developed ways of working with schools to address this problem, and to monitor children's attendance without unduly stigmatising the child. We strongly support this type of approach and would encourage authorities to work together to share effective practice in improving the attendance of children in care. Providing real stability in school must be a priority if we are to offer children in care the best possible chance of achieving.

5.31 Once children in care have been admitted to the right school for them, they should be able to stay there. Children have also told us that this is important not just for getting good exam results, but also for making friends[33].

5.32 We therefore intend to introduce measures which will deliver increased stability for children in care in schools. In order to prevent children from having to leave their existing school following a change in their care placement, we propose to:

Tower Hamlets have contracted with a private company to monitor the school attendance of their children in care. The company call the school every day for those children most at risk of non-attendance and less frequently for those attending regularly. Where a child is not in school, Tower Hamlets will be alerted the same morning and can then investigate the reasons for non-attendance. As a result, the number of children in care absent for 25 days or more dropped by 22% in a year; the number of children with fixed term exclusions dropped from by 33%; and the number of fixed term exclusions dropped by more than 50%.

---

32 Source: School Census. The data collected through the School Census is thought to under report numbers of looked after children and should therefore be treated with caution.

33 CSCI: Children's Rights Director (2006) *Children's Views on Standards*

- **Create a presumption that young people in care do not move schools in years 10-11, unless it can clearly be demonstrated to be in the young person's best interests.**

5.33 Social workers sometimes decide to move a child between schools because the cost of transport to a new placement is too high. In order to ensure that children will only move schools where it will benefit their educational welfare, we propose to:

- **Offer a free entitlement to school transport for children in care to allow children to remain in the same school after a placement move. In developing this proposal we will consider what criteria should apply to ensure that costs and travel times are limited at a sensible level.**

5.34 Exclusions from school are also a major issue for children in care. 0.9% of children in care were permanently excluded in 2004/5 compared with 0.1% of all children.

"If you're going to get excluded, there's nothing you can do."

5.35 We support the right of headteachers to exclude pupils from school and children in care must be held to the same high standards of behaviour as their peers – which means that sometimes exclusions may be unavoidable. However, we believe that it should always be the option of last resort and that for children in care in

particular, as with other vulnerable groups such as those with special educational needs, every effort must be made to intervene early and prevent behaviour reaching the threshold for exclusion.

5.36 There are excellent examples of good practice in schools and local authorities which have managed to reduce exclusions of children in care, and we would encourage other local authorities to follow this example where possible.

5.37 We also need to ensure that both schools and social workers support children as much as possible in order to prevent exclusion. Chapter 6 sets out a range of proposals for enabling foster carers and other professionals working directly with children in care to manage challenging behaviour more effectively. We would also expect all schools to have in place comprehensive behaviour management strategies, reducing the need for exclusions. Children in care exhibiting challenging behaviour benefit directly from such approaches. But children in care have told us that they are also frequently the victims, rather than the perpetrators, of bullying and aggression at school because of the stigma of being in care. Improved behaviour management strategies can therefore help to reduce the negative impacts of being a child in care at school.

Lewisham Council introduced a zero-tolerance approach to exclusions of children in care three years ago. Agreed in consultation between the Director of Children's Services and all head teachers in the area, this policy has led to there being no exclusions of children in care for two years. The policy is underpinned by the use of a range of effective behaviour improvement techniques such as restorative justice.

5.38 In order to underpin this approach, we will:

- **Strengthen existing guidance on school exclusions to encourage schools not to exclude children in care other than in the most exceptional circumstances; and**

- **Direct Government Offices to analyse differential data on exclusions of children in care across their regions, and ask Ofsted to investigate examples of poor or good practice.**

5.39 The reforms to 14-19 education will create a more collaborative system where schools, colleges and other providers work together to meet the needs of young learners. Children from the age of 14 will have opportunities to study some of the time in FE colleges and with work-based learning providers. Such experiences can in themselves help to re-engage children at risk of exclusion.

5.40 We know from Ofsted that there is a culture in some areas of 'informal exclusions'. In these circumstances children – including those in care – are discouraged from attending school without being formally excluded because schools feel they are disruptive or difficult to teach. This practice is unacceptable and local authorities and schools should work together to make sure it does not happen.

5.41 We believe that most children in care will benefit from being in a mainstream school and every effort should be made to secure a place in such a school unless it is clearly not right for the child. However, for some children in care education at a mainstream school will not be possible and they will need alternative forms of provision. This may be because of a child's disability, special educational needs, mental health difficulties or behavioural difficulties. It is essential that high quality provision is made for these children, which is appropriate to their individual needs. The Education Act 1996 makes clear that local authorities are under a duty to do so.

5.42 Local authorities have taken a range of approaches to providing alternative education, including through Further Education Colleges, work experience placements, hospital schools, teenage parents' units, home tuition or Pupil Referral Units (a type of small, specialised school for children unable to attend mainstream schools). Some children in care are also educated in children's homes which are themselves registered as schools. For some children this can be an excellent way of ensuring a good education which they would not otherwise get.

High levels of need

5.43 Some of the underachievement described above can be explained by the particularly complex needs of many children in care. 27% of children in care have a statement of special educational needs, which is known to be correlated with lower educational attainment, compared to just 3% of all children.

5.44 However, data shows that children in care do significantly worse even when compared with children with similar levels of need. For example, less than 20% of children in care with a statement of special educational needs achieved 5A*-G GCSEs in 2004 compared with 37% of all children with a statement.[34]

---

34   School Census. The data collected through the School Census is thought to under report children in care and should be treated with caution.

5.45 It is therefore critical that that every child in care is given a personalised education which suits their own particular needs. Any concerned parent with a child who experiences difficulties in obtaining the best possible support would lobby tirelessly on behalf of that child, and as corporate parent it is vital that we do the same.

5.46 However, rather than receiving a high class education designed to meet their needs, children in care have told us that they often feel stigmatised. Schools will often need to provide additional support to children in care, but this should be done in a way which does not make the child feel that they are different to their peers.

" [Schools should] treat you like any other person – they treat you differently if they know you're fostered."

5.47 Key to ensuring that the school system delivers for children in care is a thorough assessment of each individual's needs and a plan for meeting them. There are currently a range of different plans that may be used for children in care, several of which relate to education. The Personal Education Plan is an integral part of the child's Care Plan and records what needs to happen for children in care to enable them to fulfil their potential. It should reflect and refer to any other existing education plans, including the Pastoral Support Plan for children at serious risk of disaffection or exclusion, transition plans for young people with special educational needs and person-centred plans for some young people with learning disabilities.

5.48 While each of these plans has a specific purpose, the number can be confusing for children and result in a needless amount of bureaucracy. We will:

- **Rationalise the planning processes for the education of children in care so that wherever possible a single 'conversation' – review and planning meeting – is held to cover all issues and plan for the child's future education. This will be covered in new guidance.**

5.49 *Higher Standards, Better Schools for All* emphasised the importance of personalised learning, through which education is tailored to meet the needs of individual children. We have given schools an additional £990 million over the next three years to make that vision a reality for all children, funding a range of activities from intensive small-group tuition and one-to-one support for children requiring 'catch-up' lessons to additional 'stretch' and challenge for gifted and talented learners or learning mentors for those who need them.

Priory School in Portsmouth has appointed its own Educational Psychologist (EP) to address a wide range of needs in all children and specific needs in more vulnerable children, including children in care. The EP has a key role in the senior management team and, since September 2005, she has worked at a strategic level to transform the school's inclusion policy as well as working directly with teaching staff, children and parents. She conducts one-on-one and group discussions with students, provides drop-in sessions for staff and students and works with parents and carers to tackle behavioural, emotional and family problems.

5.50 It will be for schools to decide how best to use the new resources available for personalisation, based on high quality formative assessment of pupil progress. School Improvement Partners and the new Ofsted inspection regime will challenge every primary and secondary school to demonstrate that they are planning and delivering support where it is needed, with the most intensive support for those children facing the greatest disadvantages. We would expect schools to consider in particular the needs of each child in care in spending this resource. We will:

- **Continue to encourage schools to give a special priority to the needs of children in care as they spend the additional £990m personalisation funding we are providing by 2007-08.**

5.51 The way in which personalisation should support children in care will also be considered in more detail by the forthcoming review of Teaching and Learning in 2020, due to report later this year.

5.52 One key means of offering personalised support to this group of children is through the innovative use of ICT. New technologies have the potential to build stronger links between home and school, to help children learn both in and out of the school environment and to ensure continuity across key transition phases such as to post 16 education and training. We are committed to ensuring each child has a learning platform by 2008, offering a range of features such as sophisticated learning support and help for children to stay in touch with friends and family. To help ensure these work for children in care we will:

- **Pilot different approaches to building on the new investment in learning platforms, and examine how best to support children in care and their carers across a range of ages and educational settings.**

5.53 We also want to explore the potential of an on-line learning resource for children in care to provide them with a range of help with learning in a single, easily accessible place. This could be especially valuable in helping to keep young people engaged in learning. A wide range of services could be provided – structured learning materials; e-mentoring; peer networks and study groups; and services and support for carers to help them support young people's learning. We want to explore the potential of this approach, both with children in care and other groups who would benefit from additional learning support and will:

- **Investigate with the British Educational Communictions and Technology Agency (BECTA), the feasibility of an on-line learning resource for children in care.**

5.54 The reforms set out in the 14-19 Education and Skills White Paper will also bring greater flexibility and choice to the system. Young people will increasingly be able to choose a curriculum, a style of learning and even an educational setting which best meets their needs while keeping their options open regarding future study and employment. There will be greater emphasis on the core 'functional' skills of maths and English which are so important to future success. We will also be piloting a new programme at KS4 which provides a personalised approach to re-engaging

Ben was taken into care as a result of his mother's drug and alcohol misuse. After a failed return home and moving through several foster placements in quick succession, Ben was placed with his aunt and uncle. Ben had missed large parts of his GCSE coursework as a result of moving placements, but his new placement provided him with the stable base and the encouragement he needed.

Ben's social worker, after discussing it with his school, arranged for Ben to receive extra tuition in Maths and Physics, two subjects he enjoyed but struggled with. As a result of the extra support and the assistance of his carers, Ben was very successful and obtained seven GCSEs at A-C. Ben lived with his aunt and uncle during sixth form and achieved three good A-levels before going on to study history at university. Ben has no doubt that this wouldn't have been possible without the support of his aunt and uncle.

young people who have become disengaged from education as a whole.

5.55 A good parent with sufficient financial resources will support their child's education not just by sending them to a good school, but by using those financial resources to buy in additional support where necessary. In some instances this might be directly related to education, such as home tutoring in a subject which the child is struggling with at school, but in others it will enhance the child's overall intellectual and creative development, such as music lessons.

5.56 In order to ensure that as corporate parent the local authority is able to exercise similar choices for children in care, we propose to:

- **Make available a personalised annual budget of around £500 per child per year for social workers to spend on each child in care to support their education. This would be drawn from the existing Dedicated Schools Grant provided to local authorities, and would be in addition to the provision that the school would otherwise make for the child from its own budget; and**

- **Facilitate a pilot project, funded by HSBC, to provide private tutoring for children in care. Tutors would be overseen by the Virtual Headteacher (see below), and the scheme will be fully evaluated and the results disseminated to local authorities to enable them to develop their own approaches.**

5.57 We would expect the use of this personalised budget to be agreed between the social worker and the school, but also with carers and children themselves, who must be fully involved in decisions about what they need to support their learning.

5.58 It is important to have a mechanism for ensuring that every child receives the entitlements outlined in this chapter. To do this, we will strengthen the role of the Designated Teacher in each school to provide oversight and challenge.

5.59 We have already set out in guidance that schools should have a Designated Teacher who co-ordinates support for children in care. However, in practice Designated Teachers do not always have sufficient influence within the school, especially

The progress of children in care at **Robert Clack Secondary School** in Barking and Dagenham is followed closely and singled out specifically in the school's processes for monitoring academic progression. The agenda for the school's weekly Behaviour Management Group, chaired by the Head, has a standing item on children in care, at which the designated teacher reports on how they are all doing.

The Head takes a personal role in ensuring that children in care are being supported well in the school, for example meeting the foster carer of each new pupil who is in care to ensure the foster carer has confidence in the school and to explain how the school can help support the child.

where the number of children in care is small. We therefore propose to:

- **Place the Designated Teacher for Children in Care on a statutory footing, setting out clearly what their role and functions must be.**

Making sure the system works

5.60 We will consult on how this role fits with other key roles within schools, such as the SENCO, and how the role can be best exercised. This individual should ensure that the school allocates sufficient resource to children in care and should act as a key point of contact within the school for professionals and carers in the child's life. The Designated Teacher will also act as an advocate for individual children where necessary.

5.61 The home environment is the most powerful factor in determining a child's

level of educational achievement. We have already shown that many children in care are not in placements which meet their needs, and the proposals set out in Chapter 4 aim to address this.

5.62 However, even where the placement is suitable, it remains important that the child also benefits from active engagement in their education by social workers and carers.

5.63 For example, we know that many children in care do not have anyone attending parents' evenings on their behalf[35]. In the vast majority of cases, the foster carer should attend parents' evenings. For those children in residential care, the social worker must decide whether to attend him/herself or whether to delegate the responsibility to a suitable person within the residential setting.

5.64 We need to ensure that the social worker takes full responsibility for supporting the

Children in care in the Greets Green area in Sandwell have received support from a range of programmes to help raise their attainment through **Sandwell New Deal for Communities**. Activities have included tutors working with children and their carers at home, a Study Zone to support groups of young people with their GCSE coursework and visits to all schools in the area with one or more children in care to help build an understanding of their needs and how to meet them. Over 40 young people in the area, alongside schools and carers, have received support from the programme.

---

35 Barnardos (2006) *Failed by the system*

child in their education, delegating particular tasks to the carer as appropriate. Local authorities undertake this role to different degrees, and we need to spread best practice in this area more proactively.

5.65 In order to fulfil this dual role of checking that the system is delivering for children in care and identifying and disseminating best practice, we propose to:

- **Pilot the introduction of a 'virtual head teacher' in a number of trailblazer authorities, with a view to rolling out across the country if the pilots are successful.**

5.66 This Virtual Headteacher will be a senior individual working for the local authority and tasked with driving up standards in the education of children in care. They would work to support all children in the authority's care, wherever they go to school, and for children placed in their area by other authorities. We expect that this role would generally be undertaken by a former headteacher with experience of supporting vulnerable children in school.

5.67 He or she would work directly with schools and alongside School Improvement Partners to drive up standards of education for children in care as though they attended a single 'virtual school'.

5.68 Their role would include:

- Providing professional leadership and development for Designated Teachers;
- Monitoring the progress of children in care in different schools and challenging those schools where they are doing less well;
- Disseminating good practice on working with children in care;
- Running joint training events for school staff, carers and social workers to build networks around children; and
- Working with 14-19 partnerships to ensure that the needs of children in care are being met through the new, collaborative arrangements.

5.69 To help drive up levels of educational attainment for children in care, it will be important that Virtual Head teachers have access to robust information which shows an individual child's educational outcomes over time to help compare them with those of other children in care with similar backgrounds. This would identify whether individual children in care are achieving their potential or falling behind and could also be aggregated to school and local authority level and compared with relevant national benchmarks.

Liverpool Council have been running a 'Virtual School' since 2001. The Virtual School pulls together data on children in care from a number of sources to produce a regular report for senior Councillors, the Director of Children's Services, and head teachers.

The virtual school is overseen by a 'virtual head' – a former head teacher and head of a Pupil Referral Unit – as well as a number of teachers, an attendance officer, a youth worker seconded to the team, and an inclusion officer who works with children whose school placement is at risk of breaking down. The School has made significant improvements in outcomes, with 54% of children in care getting one or more GCSEs compared to 33% the year before the virtual school was introduced.

5.70 The Virtual Head will also have a role in reporting on the performance of local schools in relation to this group of children. We propose:

- **That the virtual head teacher will produce an annual Self-Evaluation Form setting out their assessment of the progress of all children in care in the area.**

5.71 The Virtual Head will provide support and challenge to local head teachers in how they provide for children in care. They will work directly with other members of schools' senior management teams who have a specific responsibility in this area including the Designated Teacher. By looking at data on the attainment and attendance of children in care and seeking feedback from schools, carers and social workers about how children in care are developing in their education and participating in wider activities, the Virtual Head Teacher will be able to identify those schools serving children in care well and those who need to improve.

5.72 We would expect the Virtual Head Teacher to get involved in local authority-wide issues relevant to education, such as ensuring foster carers are engaging with schools effectively and advising on which schools are best placed to meet the needs of individual children in care. The Virtual Head Teacher, working alongside local head teachers and through the local authority, will encourage and spread best practice but also challenge those who need to do more.

5.73 And to ensure that children in care are also high on the agenda of the governing body of each school, we also propose:

- **To develop a new, nationally available training module for governors on how schools should cater for children in care.**

Progression

5.74 The proposals set out so far in this chapter describe a school system in which children in care are supported to reach their potential. However, it is not just at compulsory school age that children in care need special attention. Children in care are also less likely to go on to further education and training post-16 than their peers, with only 19% of care-leavers in college and 6% in university at 19, compared with 38% of all 19 year olds in one or the other.

5.75 Further Education Colleges and work-based learning providers potentially offer children in care an excellent route towards education, training and employment from aged 16 onwards within institutions experienced in offering personalised education packages.

Alex had been in care since the age of four and throughout his youth had been in and out of prison. With the help of his leaving care adviser he was encouraged to join a 'Youthbuilding project' which helped young people from socially excluded backgrounds to develop their skills through work-based learning. Alex became secretary of the project and went on to gain vocational skills in mechanical engineering. Following completion of the project, he became interested in the vehicle trade and is currently an assistant manager in a large city garage.

5.76 The Learning and Skills Council have a crucial role to play in ensuring that the right learning opportunities are available locally and we will:

- **Work with the Learning and Skills Council to ensure that the needs of children in care and young people making the transition from care up to the age of 25 are taken into account in developing and delivering local learning opportunities.**

5.77 The White Paper *14-19 Education and Skills* set out an ambitious programme of reform aiming to enable all young people to stay on in education and training up to age 19. All young people will have an entitlement to study one of 14 new specialised Diplomas, giving them the opportunity to experience more practical learning, delivered in realistic settings, from the age of 14.

5.78 The more recent White Paper *Further Education: Raising Skills, Improving Life Chances* explained how the FE system would change to support that ambition. It is therefore in this context that our proposals for enabling more children in care to continue in education and training post-16 need to be set.

5.79 Children in care need the right the advice and assistance to access opportunities in FE, particularly when they have missed substantial parts of their school education. For some, that will mean picking up again or developing the basic skills they need just to get started. To help these young people we propose to:

- **Create a new entitlement for all children in care/care leavers to have access to support through a personal adviser until the age of 25. Roll out would begin in a number of pathfinder areas. This would ensure that young people could take advantage of advice and support up to the age of 25, giving them the maximum opportunity to take advantage of the new entitlement to free first-time Level 2 and Level 3 learning;**

- **Target children in care and their carers in recruitment programmes for literacy, language and numeracy skills courses; and**

- **Develop a specific Family Literacy, Language and Learning package for children in care and their carers.**

5.80 We know that the most successful schools track the progress of pupils very closely and have developed very sophisticated systems to help them do this. However, the transition of children in care from school to FE is not always supported by a good exchange of information so it is not always easy for FE providers to identify the extra support many children in care will need. To address this we will:

- **Improve the collection of data on children in care in FE colleges so that we can track participation, progression and attainment of children in care;**

- **Develop a self-assessment tool kit for FE institutions to evaluate the effectiveness of the support they are offering to children in care; and**

- **Provide that the Virtual Head Teacher role to be piloted would cover FE provision as well as school provision, challenging and supporting learning providers in how they work with children in care and care-leavers.**

5.81 Colleges and the FE sector have an excellent record in supporting young people with a commitment to learning but who need extra support to achieve their potential. We want to ensure that the particular needs of children in care are understood and prioritised across the FE sector. We will:

- **Introduce mandatory training on children in care for new FE principals, as part of their qualification criteria, and develop a Continuing Professional Development module for existing principals;**

- **Include a module within the professionalisation programme for Skills for Life professionals which will help them meet the needs of children in care; and**

- **Develop a pilot on pastoral support to help FE providers better meet the personal needs of children in care and care leavers.**

5.82 Because children in care are so vulnerable to missing parts of their schooling, it is essential that the system is flexible enough to support them in re-engaging with their learning. To help meet this need we will:

- **Explore the possibility of flexible starting dates for young people who want to pursue specialised Diplomas and other qualifications in an FE setting; and**

- **Introduce flexible learning pathways within the Foundation Learning Tier that enable young people to progress to employment or further learning and education. This will include a new pre-Apprenticeship pathway that will provide young people with a work-based learning route.**

5.83 To further strengthen the voice of children in care and care leavers within the FE sector we will:

- **Consult children in care and care leavers on the vision statement for FE, and ensure their experiences and views are represented on the FE National Learner Panel which will be launched in November.**

- **Require each FE provider to put in place a Learner Involvement Strategy that seeks and responds to the views of learners and includes the views of children in care and care-leavers.**

5.84 In our conversations with practitioners, concerns have been raised that some local authorities are providing care-leavers with lower levels of financial support when they are in receipt of the Educational Maintenance Allowance. This is inappropriate and should not be happening – a young person receiving the EMA has the right to the same level of financial support from the Local authority. We will :

- **Make clear to local authorities that they should not take the EMA into account in determining the level of financial support to be provided to a care-leaver.**

Questions for consultation

How might the role of the Designated Teacher for children in care be strengthened further?

How would a 'virtual headteacher' best raise standards for children in care?

What more can be done to reinforce the educational role of the carer?

Are the measures proposed in relation to Further Education sufficient to achieve a step change in outcomes for young people in and leaving care?

Chapter 6
Life outside school

Summary

Care should be a positive influence in a child's life, offering them all the opportunities any parent would want for their child. Children in care must have the chance to participate in sports, volunteering and the arts, and be supported to remain healthy and safe, and to avoid damaging or anti-social behaviour. All local services have a responsibility to offer the best possible support to these children, and to make sure they have access to the services they need for care to be a positive and enjoyable part of their childhood. Our proposals include:

- Encouraging local authorities to provide free access for children in care to the facilities they own and manage such as leisure centres, sports grounds and youth clubs;

- Setting out and encouraging all local areas to use a model of excellent physical and mental health services for children in care;

- Offering every child in care a named health professional to ensure their individual needs are met;

- Providing toolkits for carers and designated teachers, setting out their responsibilities for offering sex and relationship education to children in care and effective techniques for offering this education;

- Offering a Personal Adviser to every young woman in care who becomes pregnant;

- Introducing screening for substance misuse as a routine part of regular health assessments, so that young people can receive appropriate support and interventions;

- Building approaches to managing behaviour, based on evaluated practice such as restorative justice, into the framework of training and qualifications for carers; and

- Providing extra help for young people in care who enter youth custody, so that more continue to receive support, including leaving care support for older young people.

6.1 Children in care deserve to enjoy a well-rounded childhood, and to achieve all of the five outcomes underpinning *Every Child Matters*. It is the responsibility of every part of the State, as their corporate parent, to deliver this and the Children Act 2004 set out a duty on all local agencies to co-operate with the local authority to this end.

6.2 Children in care frequently have greater and more complex needs than other children, as the evidence in chapter 1 shows. But these needs are often not adequately met. Despite great progress, around one in five still do not receive a basic annual health assessment and a similar proportion do not receive regular dental check-ups (though in some cases this is because children themselves are unwilling to have these check-ups). And while only a very small number of young women in care become teenage mothers, they are three times more likely than other young women to do so.

6.3 It is critical that as their corporate parent we support children in care to flourish. We know that children in care have the same aspirations for enjoyment and fulfilment in their lives as any other child and we must ensure, for example, that our critical focus on safeguarding does not obscure all the other important aspects of children's lives.

" I did football before I was in care, but I got moved and then they said 'no' to me continuing. "

6.4 Research evidence and our discussions with local authorities and providers suggest that children in care often tend to miss out on the range of activities enjoyed by their peers. Like other disadvantaged young people, children in care are less likely to participate in sports, to visit the cinema or theatre, or to read a book for pleasure[36].

6.5 Children also need help to avoid the risk of damaging behaviour, which can result from their experiences before or after entering care. Children in care tend to start using drugs at an earlier age, at higher levels and more regularly than their peers who are not in care[37]. While only a relatively small minority of children in care offend (around 9%), it remains the case that those in care are around three times more likely than other children to be cautioned or convicted of an offence while in care.

6.6 For care to be a positive experience for children, they need the right help in all of these aspects of their lives. That help must be provided in a way which is responsive to their needs and easy to access. This requires professionals to be informed and sensitive about issues relating to race and ethnicity, sexuality, religion and disability. Children in care can enjoy a well-rounded childhood only if every member of the children's trust is prepared to work with social workers to put these children first.

Enjoying and achieving

6.7 Having "things to do and places to go" can make an important contribution to the lives of children and young people in care, not only by helping to improve educational achievement and emotional and mental health but also by increasing their confidence, motivation and enjoyment of life.

6.8 A great deal has been done to offer opportunities to participate to all young people. *Youth Matters* set out an ambitious programme for engaging more young

---

36 Department of Health Quality Protects Research Brief 4 (2000): *Value of Sport and the Arts*

37 Newburn and Pearson (2002) *The place and meaning of drug use in the lives of young people in care.*

people in their communities, and set out a commitment to implement integrated targeted youth support arrangements in all areas by March 2008.

6.9 As set out in chapter 2, targeted youth support will ensure that young people at risk and facing a number of difficulties in their lives receive a co-ordinated package of support tailored to their needs. It is critical that the needs of young people in care are taken into account in the design of local targeted youth support programmes, and that social workers and leaving care advisers are clearly connected into the framework. This will help to ensure that young people in care benefit from the increased integration of service planning and delivery that integrated targeted support offers and that there is continuity for young people entering and leaving the care system.

6.10 To inform the national move to more integrated support for young people at risk, 14 children's trusts have been participating in a one-year targeted youth support pathfinder since September 2005. A number of these pilots are focusing specifically on children in care and we will ensure that the findings are disseminated as the programme rolls out nationally.

6.11 There is also a wealth of excellent work at the local level in relation to sports and other facilities for young people:

- By 2006, the Government, with the National Lottery, will have channelled over £1 billion into refurbishing local sports facilities;

- The National School Sport Strategy aims to offer all school age young people at least two hours a week of high quality PE and sport;

- Creative Partnerships are bringing experience of arts, museums and libraries to over 610,000 children in the most deprived communities;

- We are investing over £180 million per year in programmes to engage young people in arts, music, drama and film; and

- The Youth Opportunity Fund and Youth Capital Funds are providing £115 million over two years for improving positive activities and associated facilities for young people in local areas, and we will expect children in care to have a central part in deciding how it is spent.

6.12 The impact of this investment has been achieved through the work of local authorities and their partners. They have developed a vast array of projects to help children and young people enjoy what their area and their community has to offer.

6.13 Local authorities should treat children in care as their own children. As part of that, they should be giving them the best of what the corporate parent has to offer.

Tate Britain has carried out a series of projects to engage children and young people in care in artistic and cultural activities. In one such project, children and young people worked with artists over 6 months to produce their own personalised map of London, professionally produced and showing the places that were important to them between Harrow, where they lived, and Tate Britain.

This includes considering the needs of children in care when responding to the new duty to secure access for all young people to sufficient positive activities, which will come into force in January next year.[38] In doing so, we would encourage all local authorities to:

- **Provide free access to the facilities they own and manage such as leisure centres, sports grounds and youth clubs, and to contribute to the costs of activities provided by the private or voluntary and community sector.**

6.14 We are investing up to £100 million over three years in the national framework for youth volunteering recommended by the Russell Commission, aiming to inspire and engage a million more volunteers between the ages of 16 and 25. Social workers and carers should ensure that young people in care and those leaving care access the new volunteering opportunities that will be created as a result.[39]

6.15 Local authorities should also consult with young people in care about what activities they want to take part in, and the barriers that may stop them doing so. Authorities should work with partner agencies to secure access to sufficient, appropriate provision.

6.16 In addition, to help ensure children in care make the most of the opportunities their area provides we propose to:

- **Ask local authorities to help young people in care to access information on positive activities through the new positive activities information service proposed in *Youth Matters* and required under new legislation.[40]**

- **Ask every local authority to provide a pack to carers, via social workers, setting out the activities available in their area. We would provide a national template for these packs, including vouchers and signposting to things to do and places to go; and**

The four years running up to the **London Olympics and Paralympics** in 2012 will provide a wide range of opportunities for children and young people to be involved in activities and events inspired by or in some way directly contributing to the 2012 Games. We are currently drawing up a national 2012 programme to engage children and young people in exciting educational, sporting, cultural and volunteering activities. Some elements of the programme are already underway, for example the first annual UK School Games took place in Glasgow in September 2006. It is important that children and young people from all backgrounds are involved and we will work with local authorities and schools to make sure that children in care are given priority in accessing the many opportunities within the 2012 programme to develop and make a positive contribution.

---

38 Clause 6 of the Education and Inspections Act 2006 introduced new section 507B to the Education Act 1996. 507B places new duties on local authorities regarding securing access to positive activities for young people, consulting with young people regarding positive activities and providing information on positive activities. Statutory guidance on the new duties will be published in early 2007.

39 The Russell Commission was set up in May 2004 by the then Home Secretary, David Blunkett, and the Chancellor of the Exchequer, Gordon Brown with the aim of developing a new national framework for youth action and engagement as part of the Government's commitment to increasing youth volunteering and civic service.

40 See 22 above – also guidance on the information service is contained in *The provision of information to young people regarding positive activities and associated facilities* – available from www.everychildmatters.gov.uk

Up for it! in the West Midlands provided opportunities for children in care to work with professional artists. This initiative involved pairs of artists, representing different art-forms, working in three residential children's homes on a long term basis to develop ongoing relationships with the young people aged 8 – 16 year old.

- **Disseminate the lessons from the Paul Hamlyn Foundation 'Right to Read' programme for use by all authorities.**

6.17 The Foundation has produced a checklist for local authorities on improving access to books and libraries for children in care, including:

- Library staff receiving training, including on provision of reading materials to provide the sort of educational information which children and young people may be missing if they are out of school;

- Library services being involved in training for carers and social workers. Library membership/use should be part of children's PEPs; and

- Earmarking funds to buy books for individual children in care.

Being healthy

6.18 Taking part in positive and enjoyable activities gives children a strong foundation for a healthy childhood. We know that taking part in sporting, cultural and community activities makes a real difference to children's physical and mental health. However, many children in care have additional health needs and require an effective and responsive health care system to meet them. Because of the trauma many have experienced before entering care, many children in care have particularly acute mental health problems and emotional and behavioural difficulties.

6.19 There is a strong foundation on which to build in seeking to ensure the mental and physical health needs of children in care are met:

- In 2002, *Promoting the Health of Looked After Children* set out a comprehensive health assessment which included such areas as progress at school and ability to build relationships and relate to peers;

- The *National Healthy Care Programme* helps services to focus on the four key areas of policy, partnership, participation and practice to achieve the ingredients for a healthy care environment;

- *The National Service Framework for Children, Young People and Maternity Services*, 2004 set out a number of requirements related to children in care;

- *Comprehensive Child and Adolescent Mental Health Services (CAMHS)* – we increased investment in CAHMS by over £300m to the NHS and local authorities in the period 2003-06. The Department of Health is committed to achieving the Public Service Agreement Standard of access to comprehensive CAMHS for all who need them; and

- *Health Reform in England* describes a comprehensive framework for improving delivery of NHS services in England to promote choice and better outcomes for patients.

6.20 Thanks to successful practice at local level, we have built up a clear picture of the characteristics of good health services for children in care. The challenge now is to bring all of these elements together. We will:

- **Offer a model, shown in the diagram below, of how local authorities and Primary Care Trusts (PCTs) should work in partnership to deliver excellent support to all children in care; and**

- **Update the guidance on *Promoting the Health of Looked After Children*, clarifying the functions and responsibilities of those involved in ensuring that children in care receive the health services they need.**

6.21 It includes key elements such as the provision of dedicated or targeted CAHMS and offers consultation, training and support to carers and social workers as well as direct support to children in care.

6.22 We will ask Government Offices, Strategic Health Authorities and Regional Directors of Public Health to ensure that local authorities, PCTs and all NHS providers utilise this model. The LAA may be one vehicle through which local partners agree to prioritise elements of the model. We would also expect to see it set out, for example, in Children and Young People's Plans which are now in place in every local authority. Greater funding autonomy will be offered to local areas which deliver all the elements of the model set out in the diagram.

6.23 To support Primary Care Trusts and NHS providers in delivering this model, we will:

- **Set out a firm expectation in guidance that all PCTs and NHS providers will work together with local authorities to deliver LAAs in their areas.**

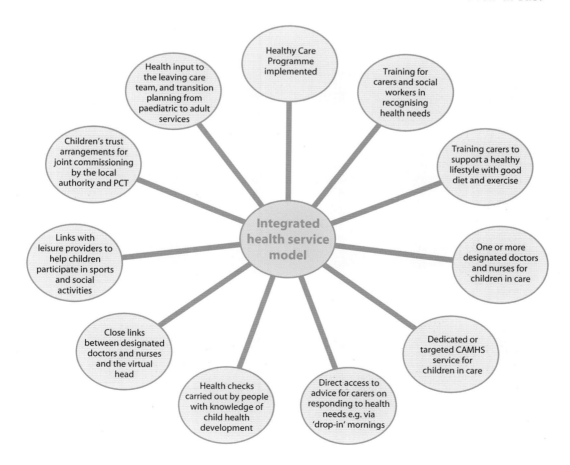

- **Ask SHAs to fulfil their role as key regional players in identifying services to improve outcomes for vulnerable groups in their areas.**

- **Highlight the comprehensive health model through the LAA toolkit hosted by IDeA and explain how it applies in relation to LAAs and local delivery plans.**

6.24 For this model to work effectively, we need every individual child to have an effective advocate within the health system as part of the core team around the child. We therefore propose that:

- **Every child in care should have a named health professional to help ensure their needs are being met.**

6.25 This person could be a doctor, nurse or other health professional allocated to the child who would monitor whether, for instance, regular health assessment and review took place. He or she would act as a single point of contact for the child, their carer and their social worker about their health needs. For many children, this might be the extent of their role but, for those who have or develop additional health needs, the named professional would become more actively involved in helping secure the right treatment and support. This role would be distinct from the existing role of the designated doctor or nurse, who assists PCTs in ensuring that services are commissioned to meet the health needs of children in care.

6.26 PCTs have an important role to play in training social workers and carers to recognise and respond to children's physical and mental health needs. In particular, both groups should be able to respond to children's emotional needs and immediate issues around attachment and loss related to entering care or changes of placement. Local authorities also have a role in commissioning such training or negotiating provision as part of children's trust arrangements. In order to facilitate this, we propose to:

- **Include specialist development modules on meeting children's physical and mental health needs in the training framework for carers and social workers.**

Promoting sexual and emotional health

6.27 Our strategy for reducing teenage pregnancy has been successful in reducing rates in most areas. Both the under 18 and under 16 conception rates are at their lowest levels for twenty years. Earlier this year we published *Teenage Pregnancy: Accelerating the Strategy to 2010* to set out how we will build on what has been achieved. There are, however, specific challenges for children in care, who are more likely than other young people to become teenage parents.

CAMHS service providers in **Darlington** have developed training courses for professionals in health, schools, and social services. The 20 week course includes techniques for assessing mental health needs and working within a multi-disciplinary team. Successful completion leads to a Certificate in Professional Development from the University of Teesside.

Bradford provides structured training to residential and foster carers, as well as to social workers, to promote an understanding of the sexual health needs of children in care, and to build the confidence of carers to talk about sexual health issues with young people. In addition, there is a dedicated leaving care nurse who works with young people aged 16 to 17 who are moving on to independent living, giving sexual health advice and facilitating a parenting group. Between 1998 and 2004, Bradford's teenage pregnancy rates fell by 22.9%.

6.28 For these children, as for others, the best form of contraception will be raised aspirations, minimising the need to turn to early sexual experiences to offer self-assurance. Beyond this, we know that areas of the country which have achieved a decline in teenage conceptions are more likely to train carers and social workers in supporting young people in care to avoid early sexual activity, advising them on contraception and supporting their emotional development. We propose to:

- **Ensure that foster and residential carers receive specific training on how to support children and young people in care to avoid pregnancy and early sexual activity, by including these issues within the new training framework set out in chapter 4;**

- **Encourage the delivery of additional training through the virtual head teacher to create a shared approach between schools, carers, and social workers; and**

- **Provide guidance for carers and designated teachers setting out their responsibilities for offering sex and relationship education to children in care; and suggesting effective techniques for offering this education and responding to questions from children.**

6.29 For those who do have children while in care, effective support must be in place. Our discussions with young people have told us that they do not always receive adequate support from their carers.

" I asked for childcare and time for myself. My foster carer says it's not her job to look after my child."

6.30 The evaluation of the Sure Start Plus pilot programme, set up to reduce long term social exclusion resulting from teenage pregnancy, showed that reintegration into school of under-16 mothers was significantly higher in Sure Start Plus areas than in matched sites. For those over 16, participation in education and training was also higher where Sure Start Plus was based in the education sector. A key success of the programme has been the role of specialist Personal Advisers who co-ordinate holistic packages of support, referring on to specialist workers such as midwives where appropriate.

6.31 It is vital that the specific needs of pregnant teenagers and teenage parents are reflected in their care plan. We will:

- **Ensure that children in care and young people making the transition from care who become pregnant have a personal adviser.**

6.32 The personal adviser will work closely with their social worker to ensure they have access to:

- Advice on pregnancy options and support in deciding what to do about their pregnancy;

- If they choose to have the child, advocacy and support during the pregnancy, and after the child is born, with healthcare, benefits, educational opportunities and childcare; and

- Advice on contraception to minimise the risk of subsequent unplanned pregnancies.

6.33 Support needs to continue throughout the young person's time in care. 80% of under-18 conceptions are among 16 and 17-year-olds, so support for those making the transition to adulthood is especially important. We will:

- **Provide guidance for local authorities on offering advice on sexual and emotional well-being and help to young parents.**

Avoiding substance misuse

6.34 We know that children in care are at greater risk than other children of becoming involved in substance misuse. Early identification of substance misuse and appropriate interventions are therefore essential to prevent problems escalating. We propose to:

- **Introduce screening[41] for substance misuse as a routine part of regular health assessments, so that young people can receive appropriate support and interventions.**

6.35 The identification and assessment of substance misuse must take place within the context of the assessment of the young person's overall needs and not as a stand alone activity. The range of interventions made available to the young person should meet this holistic assessment of need. We want to improve the ability of foster carers to recognise and respond to signs of substance misuse and propose to:

- **Include training on identifying and responding to substance misuse in the integrated training framework proposed in chapter 4.**

6.36 Where substance misuse is identified as being a concern but not the major focus, a range of interventions can be arranged by the lead professional as part of the care plan. These include drug education/harm reduction information, one-to-one support and therapeutic counselling. Targeted

Camden include substance misuse screening within the annual health assessment for children in care aged 10 or older. Social workers are receiving training in the use of a drug use screening tool which is currently being built into the social work assessment framework. To support identification of the impact of substance misuse and provide appropriate interventions, Camden has a designated young people's substance misuse worker who works with and supports looked after children both in and out of borough. All 233 children in care aged 10 and over have been screened between October 2005 and September 2006.

---

41   Drug screening is an initial assessment designed for use with children/young people about whom there may be concerns regarding drug/alcohol misuse.

support may also be required for a range of problems which may be exacerbating the young person's substance misuse, such as family contact, placement stability, school attendance or emotional and mental health problems.

6.37 Some young people with more serious substance misuse problems will need more specialist services. Where substance misuse is identified, requiring an intervention from a specialist worker focussing on a substance misuse based care plan, young people should be provided with substance misuse treatment interventions.

Avoiding crime and antisocial behaviour

6.38 Many children in care exhibit challenging behaviour, often as a reaction to the difficult circumstances which led them into care. Learning how to manage emotional and behavioural difficulties is therefore critical for both social workers and carers, and the care plan needs to set out how these issues will be managed where appropriate.

6.39 Research evidence shows a link between positive outcomes for children and carers having clear, structured strategies in place for managing behaviour, including de-escalating challenging behaviour[42]. We propose to:

- **Build approaches to managing behaviour, based on evaluated practice such as restorative justice, into the framework of training and qualifications set out in chapter 4 for foster and residential carers, including training on behaviour management strategies for managers of residential homes.**

" I want to be a nurse but I can't do it because I have a criminal record."

6.40 We have had consistent reports of children's home providers referring cases of poor behaviour to the police in response to incidents which would normally be managed within the family for children not in the care system, such as minor damage to property. To respond to this issue, we will:

- **Develop a protocol on how children's homes should work with the local police and Youth Offending Team to manage anti-social or offending behaviour by children in care, including how and when the provider will seek to involve the police.**

6.41 We will build adherence to this protocol into the revised National Minimum Standards and expect local providers to work with police services in bringing it into effect. As well as minimising inappropriate referrals to the police, this will clarify for both police and care providers how they

Hampshire Children's Services have trained all their residential staff and key stakeholders from other agencies in the use of restorative justice approaches, requiring young people who offend to meet and understand those who suffer as a result. The training programme targeted over 300 workers in 2005/06 and an additional 70 representatives from a range of agencies, including the police and magistrates, were targeted for awareness raising sessions.

---

42 Hicks et al. (2003): *Leadership and Resources in Children's Homes*

should work together to manage children's behaviour.

6.42 While we want to support all children in care to minimise and address offending behaviour, there are particular issues for children in care who enter custody. Research and data show that children in care enter custody at a far higher rate than other children and research from the Social Services Inspectorate[43] suggested that 23% of adult prisoners had been in care.

6.43 It is important that as their corporate parent, the local authority continues to take an active interest in the lives of children in care who do enter custody. Children who are in care as a result of a court-directed care order are currently entitled to this type of ongoing support. However, those who are in care through a voluntary agreement between social services and their parents lose their "looked after" status, and all the benefits which come with it, once they enter custody. Many of these children require just as much support while in custody as those in care under a care order, and we want to improve the support they receive. Therefore we propose to:

- **Require local authorities to carry out an assessment of the needs of those young people in their care on a voluntary basis who enter youth custody, with an expectation that they will continue to be supported as a child in care. In most cases this will entail a social worker, a care plan, and continued support as a child in care on leaving custody;**

6.44 A further concern is relation to children in care who enter custody is the fact that not all local authorities provide them with the full range of leaving care services including helping them to prepare for adult life. To address this we intend to:

- **Ensure that, as already required, support and preparation for adult life is provided by the local authority to young people in care aged 16 or older during their time in custody or the secure estate, just as it would be for any other child in care.**

6.45 Young people leaving care need significant support to live independently and to prepare for their adult lives, but they are not the only young people facing this situation. Young people leaving custody, or who are disabled, or estranged from their parents, or teenage parents who are unable to live with their parents or partner may also need such help. Currently, different professionals are often seeking to access or commission the same sorts of services from local agencies for such young people, yet with little interface between them.

6.46 For example, young people coming out of care are provided with services under the Leaving Care Act by local authority Leaving Care Teams, whilst young people coming out of custody are supported by resettlement workers in Youth Offending Teams, co-ordinating mainstream and specialist provision agreed through a cross-government resettlement strategy.

---

43 *When Leaving Home is also Leaving Care,* Social Services Inspectorate (1997)

6.47 We are therefore interested in exploring – through our general reforms to targeted support services for young people currently being implemented – whether more cross-cutting arrangements would improve the support available for all such young people making the transition to independent living, including those leaving care. This might include pooling budgets and resources or joint commissioning arrangements in cases where similar services are provided, such as those described above.

Questions for consultation

Have we set out the right features in the comprehensive model of healthcare for children in care?

What more could we do to help young people in care to participate in sporting, leisure and cultural activities?

Is the approach to supporting children in care who enter youth custody the right one?

What more can be done to support the role of carers in managing behaviour within the home?

Chapter 7
The transition to adult life

Summary

Many children who enter care stay for a relatively short time and leave during the course of their childhood. For older young people in care, though, the care system must provide not only a positive living environment but a bridge into adult life. It is time to leave behind the unhelpful idea of "leaving care" and recognise that every young person needs continuing help to make a smooth transition to adulthood. Any good parent continues to offer love and support to their children well beyond 18, giving them the greatest head start in life that they can. We should demand no less for young people in care. Our proposals include:

- Piloting a veto for young people in care over any decisions about legally leaving care before they turn 18, and piloting allowing young people to continue to live with foster families up to the age of 21;

- Developing training modules for carers on how to teach children and young people practical life skills;

- Improving housing options for young people through establishing a capital investment fund to support dedicated supported accommodation, underpinned by an evaluation of models of supported housing;

- Providing a top-up to the Child Trust Funds of young people in care;

- Introducing a national bursary of £2,000 for each young person in care who goes on to higher education; and

- Targeting young people in care, for example within the Aimhigher programme, to ensure they are encouraged to attend open days at higher education institutions and to take part in summer schools and other outreach work.

7.1 Too many young people in care are forced to enter adult life before they are ready. 28% still leave care at 16 at a time when most young people are focused on their education, not on having to learn to fend for themselves. Young people have told us clearly that they are not being given the kind of support they need at this age.

7.2 For too long we have used the language of young people "leaving care" between 16 and 18. For most young people the idea of being left unsupported at that age would be alien. They have a sense of security and know that their parents will always be there for them. Few young people ever really 'leave' the care of their parents. They may leave home, and on average do so at the age of 24, but they know that their families are only ever a phone call away and stand ready to offer financial support and advice, or a place to stay if they need it. Young people in care are entitled expect no less from their corporate parent and our view is that most should remain with their carers until at least 18, and beyond this age for many.

" My social worker told me that once you're 18 you can't expect any more help from social services. "

7.3 But this is not happening. A report by the Children's Rights Director on young people's views of leaving care[44] found that many young people believed that they were made to leave at the wrong time, with poor planning made for their accommodation and little practical advice.

" You are given a flat, given your money and left to get on with it. "

7.4 This picture is reinforced by data on the outcomes of young people after leaving care. While we have made great strides forward, it is still the case that only 59% of care leavers are in education, employment or training compared to 87% of all young people at 18 to 19.

Improving outcomes

7.5 There has been a huge amount of work at national and local level to improve the process by which young people in care move on to adult life. The Children (Leaving Care) Act 2000 set in place dramatic changes, giving young people an entitlement to financial assistance, accommodation during holidays from further and higher education, and access to a personal adviser to support them in education and training.

7.6 Many local authorities have gone beyond these minimum requirements to offer additional support. For instance, Ealing provide up to £5,500 a year of support for young people who go on to higher education.

7.7 The combined impact of national reforms and local good practice has led to an increase in participation in education, employment and training from 46% in 2002 to 59% in 2005. This is an improvement, but the fact remains that this leaves a vast gap between the participation rate of young people in care and that of all young people.

Entering adult life at the right time

7.8 It is enormously important to young people that they should enter adult life when they are ready. We know from research evidence both in this country and elsewhere that staying in a family environment for longer can make all the difference.

7.9 Given the choice, many young people would want to remain with a family for

44 *Young People's Views on Leaving Care: what young people in, and formerly in, residential and foster care think about leaving care,* Children's Rights Director (2006)

The **Centre for Children, University of Chicago** (May 2005) tracked 608 young people in care, and found that outcomes for young people who stayed in care up to 21 were much better than for those leaving care earlier:

- Those leaving care at 17 or 18 were 50% more likely to be unemployed or out of school than those leaving care at 20 or 21;

- Those who remained in care were much more likely to access practical support around budgeting, health, education and employment; and

- Compared to young adults still in care, the group of respondents no longer in care had higher rates of alcohol dependence, alcohol abuse, substance dependence, and substance abuse.

longer, making the bridge to independent living easier for them.

" I've said to my carer I want to stay with her for ever after I'm 18."

7.10 We want to offer young people more options, and a much greater say over becoming more independent. We want to offer them the same opportunity that all young people have to remain in a family setting and not force them to enter adult life too quickly. We propose to:

- **Pilot giving young people a veto over any decisions about legally leaving care before they turn 18; and**

- **Pilot allowing care leavers to continue to live with foster families up to the age of 21, to evaluate the support required and the impact on their longer term outcomes.**

7.11 Taken together these two proposals will offer a significant change in some young people's experience, giving them the chance to enjoy and succeed in education instead of being forced to focus on simply surviving in independent living before they feel ready to do so. Inevitably young

people living with carers for longer will add to the need to broaden the pool of potential foster carers, making our proposals on this in chapter 4 particularly important.

7.12 These proposals have implications for the way in which many local authorities organise their services for children in care. Having a 'Children in Care' team for pre-16s and a 'Leaving Care' team for post-16s, with the young person allocated to a new social worker and being prepared to leave care from the age of 16 does not provide the consistency of lead professional or the gradual approach to transition, based on the young person's preferences, that we need to see.

7.13 We must also ensure that, as far as possible, finance is not a factor for the young person in making the choice to stay with their foster family after they turn 18. We understand from stakeholders that payments made to carers in relation to young people who have legally left care are being taken into account in calculating their entitlement to benefits and that this can act as a disincentive to fostering older children in care. We are committed to removing any such barriers and will:

- **Ensure that such payments are not taken into account in calculating the carer's entitlement to benefits.**

Continuing in education, employment and training

7.14 As we saw in chapter 1, the outcomes of young people in care in later life are strikingly poor. In taking further steps to address this issue we want to build on the success of the approaches taken since the Children (Leaving Care) Act 2000 and the new entitlement for all young people to free level 2 and 3 education up to age 25. We set out in chapter 5 that we will create a number of pathfinder local authorities to give young people the right to advice from a Connexions personal adviser up to the age of 25.

7.15 This approach would provide continued access to expert education and careers advice and continued lead professional support for those who need it. In addition, we want to share what we know about the innovative practice that local authorities and voluntary and community organisations have put in place. It is important that young people are offered opportunities which will help them make a successful transition out of care, and voluntary work can offer a means to do this

while making a positive contribution to the community. We will:

- **Disseminate evidence about the outcomes of models of volunteering-based work for young people who have been in care.**

7.16 As well as these additional proposals, the approaches set out in chapter 5 to increase children and young people's basic skills are critically important. If we are to improve the life chances of young people in care we need to make sure they leave care with the skills and qualifications that employers are looking for.

7.17 One way of achieving this is for local authorities – in many places the largest employer in their area – to offer work-related placements to their own care leavers. We want to encourage all local authorities to look at this and other creative ways in which they can offer young people in their care the chance to experience a work environment, helping prepare them for the transition to adult life.

Developing practical skills

7.18 Young people in care and care leavers have told us that some of their greatest concerns about moving on to independent living are practical. They need to know how to manage on their own, whether this is about managing a budget and how to pay the rent or how to cook and clean.

Lewisham offer traineeships within council run services for young people moving on from care, giving them the chance to build up skills and experience to help secure later employment. The young people spend a year working in Environmental Services on a range of areas including plumbing, carpentry, electrical work and administration. During their year they gain a strong foundation in key skills and learn how to apply for jobs and operate effectively in a work environment. They also attend Lewisham college on day release.

> **"You should be shown how to cook and do household things, and help should be there when it is needed."**

7.19 Anecdotal evidence from our conversations with young people, carers and social workers suggests that too often this sort of education is not delivered, or is not delivered early enough. Carers' concerns about children hurting themselves while learning and uncertainty about whose responsibility it is to teach these things mean that some young people are simply not taught the basic life skills which they need to learn throughout their childhood. This may be less of a problem for those who spend a shorter period in care but for some their time in care will be their best chance to learn these skills. We therefore propose to:

- **Develop training modules for carers on how to teach children and young people about practical life skills, including how to manage this in residential homes, and what carers' responsibilities are in teaching these skills.**

Accommodation

7.20 For some young people, remaining with a foster family is not an option. These may be young people in residential care or those who simply do not want to stay in foster care. For them, supported accommodation provides an important alternative.

7.21 To increase the range of appropriate supported accommodation for young people making the transition from care, we propose to:

- **Evaluate existing models of supported housing for care leavers;**

- **Target dissemination of the results of this evaluation to local authority care leaving teams and those responsible for setting local housing priorities in order that they fully inform the next phase of local housing strategies; and**

- **Establish a capital investment fund to support the provision of dedicated accommodation.**

> **"Sleeping rough ... to grabbing a few nights kipping on a mate's floor."**

7.22 We know that young people are concerned about the risk of homelessness after leaving care. It was identified as one of their top 10 concerns in recent research by the Children's Rights Director.

7.23 Our strategy for tackling homelessness *Sustainable Communities: settled homes;*

Tower Hamlets have an agreed policy with their Housing Directorate which has allowed them to develop supported housing specifically for care leavers where they are not ready for independence, currently offering 30 places.

The range of accommodation is large, with different levels of support including some specific accommodation for single parents and disabled care-leavers. This dedicated accommodation for care leavers means that young people are with their peers and together as a group of young people with the same corporate parent, helping the local authority to ensure they are supported effectively.

changing lives recognises that young people can become homeless for a wide range of often complex reasons. We recognise that young people in care may lack the usual support networks provided by parents and friends and have a particular need for support. Since 2002, 16 and 17 year olds (with certain exceptions for young persons owed other statutory duties) and young people aged between 18 and 20 who were formerly in care have had priority need for accommodation under the homelessness legislation. This means they must be secured suitable accommodation if they become homeless through no fault of their own.

7.24 We have recently revised the Homelessness Code of Guidance for local authorities, which states that housing authorities must recognise that young people leaving care may need support and close liaison from a range of services including children's services. To complement this, we will:

- **Issue good practice guidance for children's services and housing authorities on co-operation to support young people and families with children who are homeless or at risk of homelessness.**

7.25 This will sit alongside the good practice handbook issued jointly with Centrepoint in 2002. The joint practice guidance is intended for everyone involved with the welfare of young people making the transition from care.[45]

Financial support

7.26 Despite the positive impact of the Children (Leaving Care) Act the evidence is that financial support for young people in care to enter adult life is highly variable between local authorities and often far from adequate.

7.27 Research has found that the most common weekly allowance paid across 52 leaving care teams was £42.70 and that the grant paid to young people on leaving care varied from £400 in some local authorities to as much as £2,000 in others[46]. The local authority is left to make a judgement as to the level of support required and the evidence is that young people do not always feel they get what they need.

" I lived in semi-independence with a girl from Manchester – I got £4 a week and she got £80."[47]

7.28 To improve financial support for children in care, and ensure that they have the help

Hampshire have developed a formula to determine the support they will provide for young people in care who go on to higher education. The formula takes a number of factors into account, including where in the country the young person is at university, and the cost of accommodation. Awards tend to range between £6,500 and £8,000 a year, in addition to making summer vacation work available so that young people can top up the support they receive.

---

45   Care Leaving Strategies: a good practice handbook, DTLR, DH and Centrepoint (2002)

46   *The Children Leaving care Act 2000,* Broad (2004)

47   *Young People Leaving Care: Implementing the Children (Leaving Care) Act 2000,* Broad (2004)

they need to make a successful transition to adulthood, we will:

- **Provide extra money for the Child Trust Fund accounts of young people in care. We will provide an extra £100 per year for every child who spends the year in care, in order that their Child Trust Fund provides a more significant asset for them to access on entering adult life. During the consultation period we will explore whether this is best administered through HM Revenue and Customs or by local authorities themselves.**

Increasing participation in higher education

7.29 More young people are now entering higher education than ever before. We have been ambitious in raising the participation of all young people in higher education, and we should be no less ambitious for young people in care. As things stand, only 6% enter higher education, not least because of poor attainment in school.

7.30 The problem is not just about attainment. Our conversations with young people show that many simply do not believe higher education is for them, or are discouraged because of experiences while in care.

❞ If you're excluded, they think you don't want to learn. And then you can't get into college. ❞

7.31 Young people in care can face significant barriers to entering higher education. As well as their lower attainment they lack positive role models, real encouragement to aspire to take part in what can seem a strange world, and confidence that they

will be able to meet the costs of higher education. We need to break down the barriers to entering higher education, building on the reforms we have set in place to offer better support to all those from disadvantaged backgrounds.

7.32 The University and College Admissions Service (UCAS) are plannng to introduce a tick box on their application forms so that applicants coming from a care background can be identified at the start of the admissions process and the right support can be arranged both during the admissions process and once they begin their course. This is an important step in improving support for children in care going on to university and we expect the data to be used by higher education institutions (HEIs) to monitor their progress in attracting and retaining students from a care background.

7.33 Our reforms of student finance already mean that every young person entering higher education from care will receive a non-repayable grant of £2,765 and, when charged the full tuition fee of £3070, a non-repayable bursary from their university or college of at least £305 a year. They will also have access to loans with no real terms interest to meet living costs and tuition fees, and will not be asked to pay back anything until they are working and earning in excess of £15,000.

7.34 However, we know that children in care finish higher education with an average of £2,000 more debt than their peers.[48] In order to further incentivise and support children in care to enter higher education we propose to:

---

48 *Going to University from Care*, Jackson, Ajayi and Quigley (2005)

- Introduce a national bursary, requiring local authorities to provide a minimum of £2,000 for all young people in care who go on to higher education;

- Give young people a choice of vacation accommodation, through allowing more young people to remain with carers or in accommodation in their home authority, or to remain in university accommodation; and

- Build on existing good practice targeting young people in care, for example using the Aimhigher programme, to ensure they are encouraged to attend open days, and to take part in summer schools and other outreach work.

Improving support in higher education

7.34 The introduction of the Office for Fair Access (OFFA) and access agreements within all HEIs which wish to charge higher fees has encouraged HEIs to develop further the imaginative outreach programmes which many already had in place.

7.35 We want to work with OFFA and with universities and colleges to go even further in targeting young people in care, who need the greatest encouragement and support possible if they are to fulfil their potential. We will:

- Ask OFFA to raise awareness of the under-representation in HE of children in care and to help promote the Quality Mark developed by the Frank Buttle Trust. The Quality Mark recognises HEIs that demonstrate a commitment to supporting and increasing the number of young people entering and succeeding in HE after being in care;

- Ask OFFA to consider how it can work with HEIs to improve the provision of information on bursaries, hardship grants and other financial support available to young people leaving care;

- Encourage universities and colleges to offer new undergraduates mentoring support from an older undergraduate, to help them make the transition to what will be a very new environment;

- Ask UCAS to develop and disseminate a training package for key staff in HEIs, including admissions officers and students services staff on understanding the needs of and working with young people who have been in care; and

- Encourage HEIs to have a member of staff in post with expertise in supporting care leavers, able to offer support and advice both to undergraduates and to staff working with them.

Questions for consultation

Should young people be allowed to remain with their foster families up to the age of 21, including when the young person is at university?

What is the best way of ensuring greater availability of dedicated supported accommodation for young people making the transition to adulthood?

Are there other ways in which we can increase the number of children in care progressing to university?

Chapter 8
Making the system work

Summary

The proposals set out in preceding chapters set a firm agenda for improving the outcomes of children in care. Together they equip social workers, schools and others involved with children in care to deliver radical improvements in their educational attainment. But to guarantee that these proposals will really benefit children in care we must underpin their delivery with a robust framework for ensuring that all parts of the system are genuinely held accountable. And we must be prepared to take action where children in care are not receiving the services they deserve. Our proposals include:

- Requiring Ofsted to carry out a regular inspection of how each local authority is meeting the educational needs of the children in its care;

- Introducing an annual national stock-take of the outcomes of children in care, led by Ministers and reporting to Parliament;

- Making clear in statutory guidance the responsibilities of Directors of Children's Services and Lead Members for children's services to children in care;

- Expecting every local authority to set up a 'Children in Care Council' through which children's views would be provided directly to the Director of Children's Services;

- Achieving a greater degree of autonomy for Independent Reviewing Officers, possibly through their employment by an agency external to the local authority; and

- Making the education of children in care one of the key national priorities for local government in the new national framework to be introduced in the forthcoming Local Government White Paper.

8.1 There is no doubt that there is an absolute commitment to delivering better outcomes for children in care both from national and local government and from the professionals and others working directly with children in care.

8.2 We believe that the proposals set out here will deliver radical change. But we must continually check that the system is working for these children. At every stage of delivery we must look hard at the impact on children's outcomes, recognising and spreading our successes and addressing problems robustly where they arise.

The current system of accountability

8.3   We have made real progress in recent years in delivering a system of accountability that is centred around children. *Every Child Matters* introduced a new improvement cycle in children's services, driven by the five outcomes that children have told us are important to them. Those outcomes are measured by key performance indicators and are the basis for cross-cutting Joint Area Reviews (JARs) and annual performance assessments.

8.4   The improvement cycle offers an important set of levers and incentives through which to achieve more. A better dialogue between central and local government is being facilitated through annual "Priorities Meetings" with regional Government Offices, and Local Area Agreements and Children and Young People's Plans offer a way to incentivise local solutions to problems.

8.5   However, these mechanisms are not working well enough for children in care. Local authorities, schools, and other children's trust partners need a clear picture of how well they are supporting children in care if they are to respond

effectively and have clear levers to address problems where they arise.

8.6   While the performance management regime described above has significant leverage over local authorities, as the diagram overleaf sets out there are currently limited levers over other children's trust partners to deliver good outcomes for children in care. Those levers which do exist tend to be in the form of influence rather than anything more robust.

8.7   Within this framework there are some real difficulties which need to be addressed if accountability for the outcomes of children in care is to be both strong and universal.

8.8   An examination of the results of the first JAR reports shows that while children in care are at the heart of the key judgements around which those reviews are based, their outcomes are considered only at a high level in JARs, with no real depth of analysis.

8.9   Analysis of inspection data shows that there is no statistical correlation between the outcomes of children in care and the star ratings of local authorities, whether overall or for children's services specifically. The comparatively small numbers of children in care mean that the overall rising tide of attainment can mask their poor outcomes, resulting in an authority doing

Wirral Council has a database of information on children in its care whether placed in the Wirral or outside. The data is shared with other services which input information covering attainment and other basic care information such as care order details or dates of Personal Education Plan meetings. The database has a set of 'urgencies' or flags that are used to prioritise interventions. Categories include how well a child or young person is engaging with their education placement, their attendance record, and their progress overall.

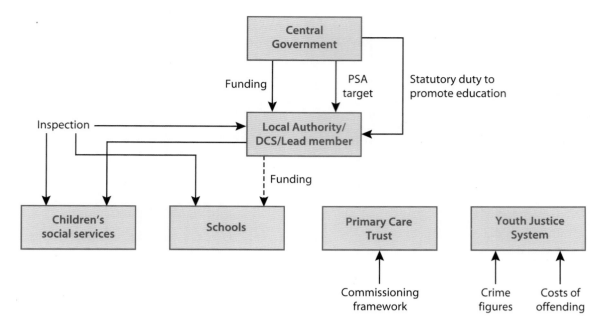

well overall despite these children's poor performance.

8.10 Similarly, children in care can be invisible in school performance tables. The majority of schools do not have more than a handful of children in care, if any, meaning that they will have almost no effect on performance tables or, in many cases, the results of inspection by Ofsted.

8.11 Children have told us that their voices are not heard clearly enough in key decisions about their care. The introduction of Independent Reviewing Officers has been a step in the right direction, but our discussions with children suggest that we still have a long way to go.

" There's not enough say about care."

"This is the first time it's happened, that I can talk about it."

(Quotes from children in care when asked at a focus group how often they were asked for their views)

8.12 Finally, we know that our current national approach to setting targets has not been effective enough. At present, 65% of children in care for 2½ years or more have been in a stable placement for at least two years, or placed for adoption. That remains a long way short of the 80% that we have set as a Public Service Agreement target. There are also concerns that this target, and other indicators on educational attainment, only offer incentives to focus on children who have been in care for a long period, and who have a chance of gaining good GCSE results. As part of the Comprehensive Spending Review we will look carefully at the overall national and local framework for setting and monitoring indicators of performance.

Better accountability at local level

8.13 We need to give local authorities a more realistic assessment of – and the public a clearer judgement on – how they are meeting the needs of children in care relative to their peers. As things stand, the lack of relationship between the outcomes of children in care and star ratings means that Directors of Children's Services can find themselves under pressure to prioritise other things over this group.

8.14 The forthcoming Local Government White Paper will set out new arrangements for assessment and inspection of local authority functions. These will be more risk-based and proportionate. However, the poor outcomes of children in care, as well as the unique nature of the State's relationship to them, require us to increase the focus on them in inspections. We will:

- **Ask Ofsted to carry out a three year programme of proportionate inspection of how each local authority is performing in relation to the education of children in care. We will review the need for further rolling inspection in this area at the end of this programme.**

8.15 The inspections will be in line with the school inspection cycle and will draw together information on children in care in all schools in the local area as well as those placed in other areas by the local authority, offering an in-depth assessment of the authority's overall performance. The reports will also include examples of individual schools doing especially well, or poorly, for children in care.

8.16 In the period up until introduction of the proposed new Local Government White Paper assessment and inspection framework, children in care inspections will feed into existing JAR judgements, and therefore feed into the Comprehensive Performance Assessment.

- **In addition to this report of local performance, we will draw together information from all areas, including children's views, in an annual national stock-take, led by Ministers, of the educational outcomes of children in care. The report of the stock-take will be laid before Parliament.**

8.17 The stock-take will recognise and celebrate the good practice of the best performers, and identify areas where improvement is needed.

Local roles and responsibilities

8.18 The improved feedback and accountability mechanisms set out above are intended to give local authorities a much clearer picture of their own performance and an idea of what effective practice is taking place elsewhere.

8.19 In each local area, it will be for the Director of Children's Services (DCS) to interpret and make use of this information. More than any other member of local authority staff the DCS must have a sense of personal responsibility for all of the children in the authority's care.

8.20 It is the DCS, alongside the lead council member for children's services, who comes closest to embodying in a single individual the role of corporate parent for all of a local authority's children in care. Our conversations with Directors of Children's Services have shown us that many already take these children's outcomes highly personally, and regard them as their own children. We strongly support their approach. We will:

KEY ROLES AND RESPONSIBILITIES

The DCS – prioritising children in care across children's services; undertaking regular reviews of individual children's progress; supporting and challenging schools on how they are driving up children's achievement; implementing statutory guidance on the duty to promote the educational achievement of children in care; securing an appropriate range of placements; working with other authorities to ensure children placed out-of-authority are supported; working with partners in the Children's Trust and beyond to improve outcomes; monitoring the performance of local authority professionals in delivering services for children in care; and appointing a suitably qualified "virtual school head".

The Lead Member for children's services – supporting the DCS in all of the above; holding him/her to account for his/her performance in carrying out those functions; making direct contact with children and actively seeking their views; championing children in care with other agencies; and holding political accountability for delivering good services and outcomes for children in care.

- **Set out in statutory guidance to Directors of Children's Services and Lead Members for children's services their responsibilities as corporate parent for children in care.**

8.21 Some local authorities have taken specific steps to bring corporate parenting alive across the whole organisation – including in those parts of the local authority who would not consider children in care part of their day-to-day business. For example, Barnet have done this by asking senior officers to champion the cases of individual children and to track their progress.

Ensuring priority in schools

8.22 In chapter 5 we proposed a new role for a virtual head teacher in each local authority who will support and challenge schools in offering the best possible support for children in care.

8.23 We need also to consider how we will help make children in care a priority for schools despite the small numbers in any one school, and encourage schools to share a sense of contributing to the corporate parenting of the child.

8.24 Some schools already do this well, taking steps to meet the additional needs of children in care and to work in partnership

Barnet has introduced a system of 'Education Champions' for children in care. Each young person in care in year 11 is assigned to a senior official within the authority, such as the Chief Executive, Chief Officers, or Assistant Directors. The scheme also includes headteachers and the Principal of the sixth form college. The 'champion' does not meet the child directly, but asks the social worker the questions that any responsible parent would ask – "why hasn't he/she been entered for this exam"? or "Why aren't they getting additional support?" The officers are asked to have the same expectations as they would for their own children, and the scheme reflects the fact that children in care themselves have said that people have been kind but tend to have low expectations.

with social workers and carers. There are others, though, who do not see these children as a priority and allow them to drift while others in the school receive better support.

8.25 For those schools where that is the case we want local authorities to take decisive action, from their perspective both as children's services authority and the corporate parent for these children. We propose to:

- **Ask Ofsted to pay particular intention in school inspections to how the needs of children in care are being met;**

- **Ensure School Improvement Partners (SIPs) provide effective challenge to schools whose performance data suggests the needs of children in care are not being adequately met;**

- **Encourage the local authority, where concerns about a school are raised by children, carers or social workers, to raise their concerns with Ofsted who will, subject to the progress of the Education and Inspections Bill, have new powers to investigate complaints and take appropriate action; and**

- **Explore the introduction of a new power by which local authorities could issue a warning notice to a school that fails to respond to challenge from the SIP or virtual head about the poor performance of the children in care at that school.**

8.26 Where such a notice is issued, the virtual head would play a role in supporting the school to make the necessary improvements. As a last resort, the authority would have a power to intervene either to appoint a new governor with specific responsibility for children in care or to require the school to take a partner, which could be a better performing school or a consultancy.

A greater voice for children

8.27 While ensuring the right levers and incentives exist throughout all parts of the system is key, it is equally vital that children themselves are able to hold the system to account.

8.28 Children have told us quite clearly that it is important to them to be listened to and to have a voice in the care they receive.

"Young people should have just as much say in their lives as adults"

8.29 The Independent Advocates discussed in chapter 3 will provide an excellent route through which children in care can express their views. As that chapter set out, Independent Advocates will act not only as friends and mentors to children in care; they will also challenge social workers, carers and other professionals and non-professionals in the child's life where the child feels that they are not receiving a proper service. By attending statutory reviews, the Independent Advocate can speak in support of the child during discussions about placement moves and other key decisions in the child's life.

8.30 We propose to build on some of the best practice in local authorities to offer a national approach based on what we know works well for children. We will:

- **Expect every local authority, as part of the pledge set out in chapter 1, to set**

The Improvement and Development Agency (IdEA) and the Local Government Association have produced a toolkit for lead council members for children entitled *Show Me How I Matter: A guide to the Education of Children in Care*. The guide sets out the responsibilities of councillors as corporate parents for these children, and the imperative to seek the same for them as any parent would for their own child. It offers guidance for local authority overview and scrutiny committees on where their focus should be in seeking the best educational outcomes for children in care.

up a 'Children in Care Council', made up of a rotating group of children in care, through which children's views would be collected and passed directly to the DCS. The views collected by this council would inform the annual national stock-take proposed in this chapter; and

- **Ask every DCS to develop an annual feedback mechanism, working alongside the Children in Care Council, to ensure that every child has the opportunity to provide their views to the DCS.**

8.31 We will ask local authorities, as part of our annual stock-take, to set out what children have told them, the action they have taken as a result, and how they have responded to children and young people. We believe that children should know what has been done in response to their views or why things they have asked for may not be possible.

Independent Reviewing Officers

8.32 In September 2004 we introduced a new role for Independent Reviewing Officers (IROs) to chair regular reviews for children in care and to bring more independent scrutiny to the process.

8.33 IROs are local authority employees but must be independent of the child's social worker's line management chain. While the role is still new, there have been real concerns raised with us about its independence since the IRO remains an employee of the local authority and some children feel it would be better placed elsewhere.

" [They] should be independent 'cos they won't be going behind your back.*"*

(Quote from a young person in care when asked if the IRO should be employed by the local authority or not)

8.34 This view is supported by the fact that so far no IRO has sought to exercise their powers to refer cases to the Children and Family Court Advisory and Support Service (CAFCASS) where there are serious concerns. We therefore want to:

- **Achieve a greater degree of independence for IROs and are seeking views through this consultation on how that can best be done, including the option of IROs being employed by an independent agency instead of the local authority.**

Monitoring our performance in future

8.35 The forthcoming Local Government White Paper will set out our proposals for a revised national framework for setting targets and expectations and for providing the right incentives for local areas to meet them.

8.36 The framework will build on the experience of local Priorities Meetings and Local Area Agreements to date, further improving the central and local government relationship, enhancing efficiency and strengthening partnership working and local authorities' community leadership role.

8.37 At the heart of the new arrangements will be a smaller, more focused set of core national priorities. We propose:

- **To make improved outcomes for children in care one of these national priorities, recognising the special responsibility of the state towards this group of children.**

8.38 We believe that our measures of outcomes in delivering against that priority must be unashamedly focused on education. Children's educational success is the best proxy we have for later life chances and is the key to improved outcomes in adult life.

8.39 There are questions, though, about the best way to measure that success:

- **Attainment** – Measures of attainment, such as the proportion sitting one or more GCSEs, or achieving a given level at Key Stage 2, are clear and easy to assess. However, the complex needs and poor life experience of children in care mean that even a lower grade at GCSE may represent immense progress while in care, and such measures may not be sophisticated enough to capture this achievement.

- **Progress** – Measures of progress, on the other hand, such as improvement across National Curriculum levels between one Key Stage and another, give a better indication of children's improvement, but are more complex to measure and interpret.

8.40 We are proposing to provide young people in care with greater support and opportunity to make a successful transition to adulthood and we must look beyond school and to longer term outcomes to measure our success in doing so. We will need to consider what information is needed, at both national and local level, to measure the outcomes of young people in adulthood – for example, at the age of 25 – and to consider how these could be built into the accountability framework of local authorities, schools and others.

8.41 Through this consultation, we want to begin a debate on what approach we should take and what our measures should be, both at national and local level. We want that debate to encompass not only what the core education measures should be, but also if and how we should measure other key factors such as children's health, wellbeing or participation in positive activities such as sports or volunteering.

Questions for consultation

Should we introduce a new power for local authorities to intervene in schools performing poorly for children in care?

What more should we do to give children in care a greater say in decisions which affect them?

How can IROs be made more independent and their role strengthened?

What key outcomes should we measure to assess whether we are being successful in transforming the lives of children and young people in care?

Chapter 9
Delivering our vision

9.1 This Green Paper has set out an ambitious vision for radically improving the outcomes of children in care and a roadmap for getting there.

9.2 We now want to hear your views on this vision and on how we can ensure that outcomes really are transformed for children in care. We want to hear the views of everyone who shares our commitment to improving outcomes for children in care and we particularly want to hear from children and young people who are or have been in care. We are publishing alongside the Green Paper a "Children and Young People's Guide to the Green Paper" which we will be disseminated to as many children and young people in care as possible.

9.3 We are offering a range of ways to respond to enable all those with an interest to take part in this consultation and allow us to consult as broadly as possible:

● You can fill in the enclosed response form and post it back;

● You can fill the form in online at www.dfes.gov.uk/consultations;

● We are making available a PowerPoint pack that anyone can download and use to help them consult others;

● We will be holding workshops to get a range of different views.

9.4 The consultation period will run from 9th October until 15th January.

Active consultation

9.5 While written responses are important and will be analysed carefully, we do not intend this to be a passive consultation. We are keen for the next three months to see active engagement across the country in firming up the ideas in this Green Paper.

9.6 Our proactive consultation strategy will focus on reaching as much of the general public and as many groups with a specific interest as possible, and on ensuring that we cover all aspects of the Green Paper. Our goal is to raise awareness of the Green Paper, to go out to every interested party to listen to their views and to speak directly to key audiences and stakeholders in every region.

9.7 The proposals in this Green Paper are wide-ranging and will impact on many groups in society, from children in care and other vulnerable children, social workers and carers, to schools and health professionals. We want to speak to all these groups to hear their views so that they can be a part of transforming the futures of children in care.

9.8 So alongside the Green Paper the Secretary of State for Education and Skills, Alan Johnson, is writing to all local Councillors urging them to look again at how they can better support children in care, and to all MPs encouraging them to use their role to improve the lives of this group.

9.9 We will also be actively consulting on a regional and national basis, working with a range of partners in the public, voluntary and community sectors to arrange seminars and conferences in order to spread our ideas and hear more about yours. A whole host of events are being organised, including the following:

- The Children's Rights Director is organising discussion groups to get the views of children in care and care leavers;

- Ministers will speak to groups of local authorities, SHA and PCT chief executives and Directors of Children's Services about how to ensure these proposals genuinely transform outcomes;

- We will run a series of consultation events and roadshows across the country to find out first hand what people think. These will provide us with the views of different groups of people from all regions of England;

- All DfES Ministers will be travelling around the country to talk to children and young people, as well as carers and social workers, about their views on the proposals in the Green Paper; and

- We will be running focus groups and workshops throughout the consultation period to get the views of various groups on the Green Paper.

9.10 And in order to explore some of the big ideas in this Green Paper in more detail, we are setting up four working groups of interested stakeholders covering the following areas:

- **Future of the care population** – this group will seek to develop the ideas floated in Chapter 2 about the need to develop a vision of the future care population.

- **Social Care Practices** – this group will examine the idea set out in Chapter 3 of local authorities contracting with independent practices of social workers to run services for children in care.

- **Placement reform** – this group will develop in more detail the proposals set out in Chapter 4 on reforming both foster and residential care, and examine the characteristics of excellence in both.

- **Best practice in schools** – building on the proposals set out in Chapter 5, this group will look at ways of ensuring that all children in care receive the best possible education and how getting this right for this most socially excluded group of children can act as a litmus test for improving outcomes for all vulnerable children.

9.11 All four working groups will be asked to report to the Secretary of State in Spring 2007 in order to inform the Next Steps document discussed below.

Next Steps

9.12 We value your responses to this document highly, and we will take into account the views which you give us during the consultation period. After the consultation we will publish an initial response document, including a version for young people, final decisions on proposals with cost implications from 2008/09 onwards will be taken in the context of the 2007 Comprehensive Spending Review. We will also announce those local authorities which have been identified as "Beacon Councils" in relation to services for children in care. These authorities will be chosen to act as centres of excellence in delivering the vision of local service delivery outlined in this Green Paper.

9.13 The case for new and ambitious action is clear. To make sure that we succeed in transforming outcomes for children in care, the new measures we take forward following consultation will need to be introduced in a coherent and manageable way, with as much flexibility for local authorities and their partners as possible.

9.14 We will address the issue of managing delivery in our Next Steps document. Our final delivery plan and timetable for reform will take account of how we can make the change programme workable for local authorities and their partners, and will be in keeping with our ambitions for local government to be set out in the forthcoming Local Government White Paper.

9.15 The proposals in this paper set out a programme of significant change in the way we work with children in care. We want to hear your views on how we should deliver our ambitions, and what else we should be doing. We are determined to make a difference to children in care, and will do so only through a passionate commitment to a vision driven by all those who work with these children in any capacity and at any level. The responsibility we have for these children makes it especially important that this is a shared vision for change, and we look forward to working with you to make that vision a reality.

Annex A
Children's views on care

A.1 Children in care have strong views about how they should be looked after and what they want to achieve. They want to enjoy a happy childhood and look forward to a positive future.

" My ambition is to become a doctor. I know that I need to work hard in my studies to get there."

A.2 Their views have been at the centre of our thinking in developing the proposals in this Green Paper, which reflect what children themselves have told us they want and need. This annex sets out the key messages from our conversations with them. In doing that, it draws on:

- Focus groups and text surveys of children in care held as part of developing policy within this Green Paper, including specific groups with children with disabilities and children from black and minority ethnic families;

- Reports and consultations by the Children's Rights Director; and

- Independent research and consultation with children and young people who are or have been in care.

A.3 The message that came through consistently and powerfully is that these are children like any others. They have the same ambitions, and the same need for a secure and positive environment at home and at school, as every child.

" I want to be a mum but I also want to be famous. I know it sounds stupid but what is what I would like. I would like to be an actress, singer or model but I'm just hoping that if I have enough determination then something will come up."

Key messages from children

A.4 As a group, children in care believe that things can be better. They have told us that care has made a difference to their lives, but also that it should be different in future. Many say that they want to become social workers or foster carers themselves and believe that their experience would let them do better for children in future.

" I want to work with children and young people who have grown up with the same or similar situation as me."

A.5 In all of our conversations with children, and in the research and other evidence we have seen, there are a number of points that come up again and again as important to children in care. These are:

- Children in care want to be treated as individuals, listened to, and helped to realise their ambitions.

- Social workers should listen to children more, and take their views seriously in key decisions.

- Children want an ordinary, supportive school experience, and don't want to be stigmatised or singled out because they're in care.

- Young people want more support leaving care, and more choice about when and how they leave.

A.6 These are the messages that have been at the forefront of our minds in building our strategy for transforming the outcomes of children in care. They are what children have told us matters most to them. But there is a great deal more that is important to children and which has informed our thinking in every part of this Green Paper.

Children on the edge of care

A.7 Children told us that more effort needs to be made to deal with family problems so they don't need to come into care, and that listening to children more could make all the difference.

" If there are problems – solve them."

A.8 Some children felt that they and their families had not had nearly enough help or warning before they came into care. Others had more positive experiences of receiving counselling and meetings with social workers. Children also felt that they should have had more help with the process of entering care and adjusting to the change in their lives.

" Most people don't even know they're going into care."

A.9 Children told us that they need better and more seamless help before, during and after their time in care. Some said, for instance, that it would help for people to be able to spend some of their time with foster carers, and some with their parents.

The role of the corporate parent

A.10 Children and young people in care felt strongly that the social worker is an important person in their lives, and should be there to offer them help and support. They felt that social workers change too often and as a result they can lack a consistent person in their lives. They told us that their three biggest wishes about social workers are:

- that they should help with personal problems;

- that they should get you practical help when you need it; and

- that they should always be there to listen to children.

A.11 There is no doubt that good social workers make all the difference. Children who have a good relationship with their social worker are very positive and say that the social worker helps them a great deal. The important thing is for social workers to be consistent, to have a personal relationship with the child, and to be someone they can turn to when they need help.

" My social worker is great. She knows lots about children with disabilities like me."

Ensuring children are in the right placement

A.12 Children believe, rightly, that their placement should provide them with a safe and happy home while they are in care.

" You should be able to talk to foster parents about problems just like your Mum and Dad."

A.13 But they told us there are some real problems with how placements work now. Many had been through a series of placements, and felt that social workers and carers didn't always listen to them or put their needs first. There were a number of key messages from children about what we need to address in order to improve placements:

- Children want a choice of placement while in care, and a backup option available if things go wrong.

- You can have a good or bad social worker, or a good or bad placement, regardless of how many "stars" your council has got.

- Ensure that the police are not involved following incidents in children's homes when they would not be involved if it happened in a domestic home – for example, many young people break things in a temper, but those in homes may get a criminal record for it.

- Foster carers need more specific training in supporting children who may need special help with particular issues or problems.

- Foster carers should be able to make all the usual decisions that parents make, as long as they keep to the agreed care plan – they should not need the social worker's approval about things like staying overnight with friends, or going on a foreign holiday as a family.

A first class education

A.14 Young people in care were positive about school, and believe that education is important to their future. However, they felt that they are often singled out in school because they are in care and that a lack of understanding from teachers and support from social workers and carers can add to the problems they face in education.

" My maths teacher told my whole class that I'm in care."

A.15 Children told us that schools should not be made to feel different from other children and that schools need to have a greater understanding about being in care. Some children had met their designated teacher and were aware of them as a source of help, but many didn't know that such a person existed at all.

A.16 Children felt that there was much more schools could do to help them stay in and get the most from school. Children suggested that they should have tutoring in and out of school, that they need more help to minimise bullying because of being in care, and that schools need to understand them and be patient with them. Many children told us about being singled out at school in an unhelpful way, such as being pulled out of lessons for review meetings or to see social workers.

Life outside school

A.17 Having an enjoyable and positive experience of life outside of school is just as important to children in care as any other child. Some children were very positive about what care offered. They felt it gave them a sense of freedom and safety they hadn't had at home, and for some it offered real differences like a clothing allowance and choice over how to spend their time.

A.18 Some children felt that they had fewer opportunities to take part in activities outside school as a result of being in care. Some told us that they had to give up hobbies and activities that were important to them because of a change of placement.

" [I want] to be able to join clubs and stay there, even when you move."

A.19 Children believe that carers and social workers should make a special effort to help them take part in positive activities.

" I live in a cottage in the countryside and I can't get lifts at night, and I can't drive. There should be more transport if you don't live in a town."

The transition to adult life

A.20 Young people in care have mixed views about their future. Some are ambitious and hopeful about what they might one day achieve but others have real worries about the impact their childhood experiences could have on their future.

" [Young people should have] a roof over their head until they've sorted themselves out."

A.21 In our conversations with children in care, younger children were more likely to be optimistic about their future and to expect to go on to university of further education after finishing school. Older children were often uncertain about what they would do after leaving care, or how they would support themselves.

A.22 The key messages from young people about entering adult life that emerged through research and our discussions with them were that:

- Young people leaving care feel they are not supported well enough, and can't cope with work and education at the same time as learning how to manage money and fend for themselves.

- Young people should leave care when they are ready, not at a particular age, and that the right support should be there when they do.

- Young people should be able to stay with their foster carers after leaving care and be able to return to them after they have left, just like other young people do with their birth families.

Annex B
Glossary of key terms

CAFCASS – The Children and Family Court Advisory and Support Service (CAFCASS) was established on 1 April 2001 as a dedicated national service to promote the best interests of children involved in family court proceedings.

CAMHS – Child and Adolescent Mental Health Services refers to the broad concept of all services that contribute in some way to the mental health care of children and young people, whether provided by health, education, social services or any other agency . This embraces universal services, such as those provided by GPs and school nurses for example, as well as more specialist services dedicated solely to the treatment of children with mental health problems.

Care – For the purposes of this document, a 'child in care' includes all children being looked after by a local authority, including those subject to care orders under section 31 of the Children Act 1989 and those looked after on a voluntary basis through an agreement with their parents.

Care order – A care order is a court order (made under section 31 of the Children Act 1989) that places a child compulsorily in the care of a designated local authority, and enables the local authority in whose favour the order is made to share parental responsibility with the parent(s). The court may only make the order if it is satisfied that the child is suffering, or is likely to suffer, significant harm; and that the harm (or likelihood of harm) is attributable to the care given to the child, or likely to be given to the child, if the order was not made, or is attributable to the child being beyond parental control.

Care plan – Following an assessment that a child needs to enter care, the social worker must ensure that the child's needs (and the services to meet those needs) are set out in a care plan. A care plan should be drawn up before the child becomes looked after, or in the case of an emergency entry to care, within 14 days. The care plan should be the basis of the plan presented to a court in cases where a local authority applies for a care order. The care plan includes key documents, such as the health plan and the personal education plan. In this document 'care plan' refers also to the ongoing plan for meeting the child's needs which is maintained while they are in care.

Children's trust – Children's trusts bring together all services for children and young people in an area, underpinned by the Children Act 2004 duty to co-operate, to focus on improving outcomes for all children and young people.

Choice Advice – The White Paper *Higher Standards, Better Schools for All* proposed the introduction of dedicated choice advisers to help less well off parents exercise their choices around the school their children attend

Commissioning – Commissioning is the systematic process of specifying, securing and monitoring services to meet identified and prioritised needs, including both immediate and anticipated needs.

Common Assessment framework – The common assessment framework (CAF) can be used as an assessment tool by the whole children's workforce to assess the additional needs of children and young people at the first signs of difficulties. The framework provides a mechanism that any practitioner working with children can use (or have access to) to identify unmet needs, so as to prevent a child's needs becoming more serious.

Corporate parent – The concept of corporate parenting was introduced when the government launched its Quality Protects initiative in 1998. In broad terms, the principle is quite simple: that as the corporate parent of children in care, a local authority has a legal and moral duty to provide the kind of loyal support that any good parents would provide for their own children. In other words, the local authority must do at least what a good parent would do. Corporate parenting also emphasises that it is the local authority as a whole, not just its social services department, which has responsibility for that child.

CSCI – The Commission for Social Care Inspection was launched in April 2004 as the single, independent inspectorate for all social care services in England, including children's services. It has three main functions: regulating care services, assessing and inspecting local

authority services, and helping support improvements in those local authority services.

Dedicated Schools Grant – The Dedicated Schools Grant (DSG) is a ring-fenced grant from the Department for Education and Skills to local authorities to cover funding delegated to individual schools, and other provision for pupils made by the local authority (such as early years provision in private, voluntary and independent settings).

Designated teacher – Schools are expected through guidance under the Children Act 2004 to appoint a designated teacher responsible for co-ordinating all of the school's services and its approach for children in care.

Director of Children's Services – Every top tier local authority in England is required to appoint a Director of Children's Services under section 18 of the Children Act 2004. Directors are responsible for discharging local authority functions that relate to children in respect of education, social services and children leaving care.

Early Years Foundation Stage – The Early Years Foundation Stage (EYFS) will provide a statutory framework to deliver improved outcomes for all children across every area of Learning and Development and to help close the achievement gap between disadvantaged children and others. EYFS sets out a universal set of requirements for all early years providers who must register with Ofsted, and for independent, maintained, non-maintained and special schools with provision for children from birth to the end of the August after their fifth birthday.

EMA – The Education Maintenance Allowance (EMA) provides a financial incentive for young people to stay on in education post-16.

Extended schools – Extended Schools offer a range of services and activities, often beyond the school day, to help meet the needs of children and young people, their families and the wider community. Possible examples of extended school activities include support for family learning; access to ICT equipment and software outside school hours for adults and pupils; and breakfast and after school clubs.

Foster care – Foster care refers to a type of placement in which the child lives with an individual in their family home. Foster carers must be approved by fostering services registered with the Commission for Social Care Inspection.

Foundation Degree – Foundation Degrees are vocational higher education qualifications, designed to provide specialist knowledge and employability skills as well as the broader understanding that equips graduates for future professional development.

Government Office – Regional offices of central Government, responsible for working with local authorities to agree priorities and communicate messages to and from central Government Departments. Government Offices are appointing Directors of Children and Learners to look across children's services.

Higher Education Institution – Refers to an organisation delivering higher education, including universities and colleges which deliver higher education as part or all of their function.

Independent Reviewing Officer – Independent reviewing officers are registered social workers who are independent of the management of the cases of children in care that they review. From September 2004, independent reviewing officers have been required to chair all statutory review meetings for children in care, from which position they

can identify any problems in the child's care and any lack of clarity in the care plan.

Integrated Children's System – This is a systematised approach for gathering and recording the information needed for the case management of social services for individual children. It includes key processes of identification, assessment, planning and review. It is based on a conceptual framework that examines a child's developmental needs, the parenting capacity available, and environmental factors.

Joint Area Review – JARs draw together a range of inspection findings to assess how services taken together contribute to improving the well-being of children and young people in a local authority area. All 150 children's services authority areas in England will receive a JAR between September 2005 and December 2008.

Lead professional – The term 'lead professional' refers to a role rather than a specific profession. For a child in care the lead professional will almost always be the social worker. They will act as a single point of contact that children, young people and their families can trust, and who is able to support them in making choices and in navigating their way through the system.

National Minimum Standards – The National Minimum Standards set out the minimum that is expected of providers of specific services, such as fostering services and children's homes. They are supported by regulations made under the Care Standards Act 2000.

OFFA – The Office for Fair Access was established under the Higher Education Act 2004 to safeguard and promote fair access to higher education. It is responsible for approving 'access agreements' proposed by higher education institutions setting out how they will support fair access based on academic merit for children from all parts of society.

Ofsted – The Office for Standards in Education is a non-ministerial government department, established under the Education (Schools) Act 1992, to take responsibility for the inspection of all schools in England. Its role also includes the inspection of the education departments of local authorities, teacher training institutions and youth work. During 2001, Ofsted became responsible for inspecting all 16-19 education, and for the regulation of early years childcare, including childminders. Under the Children Act 2004, Ofsted is to take the lead in developing a framework for integrated inspections of children's services, working alongside the Commission for Social Care Inspection, the Healthcare Commission, the Audit Commission and other inspectorates, to determine arrangement for bringing together joint inspection teams.

Out of authority placement – Refers to an arrangement in which a child is placed in a location outside the boundaries of the local authority which is its corporate parent. In these circumstances the placing authority is required to notify the authority in which the child is placed so that arrangements to meet the child's needs can be met.

Parental responsibility – Section 3 of the Children Act 1989 defines parental responsibility as all the rights, duties, powers, responsibilities and authority which, by law, a parent of a child has in relation to the child and his property. Local authorities share parental responsibility with the birth parents for children in care under a care order. Their birth families retain responsibility for those in care under a voluntary arrangement.

Pathway plan – The Children (Leaving Care) Act 2000 introduced a new duty on local authorities to support looked after young people beyond the age of 16. The plan must set out the services and the practical and emotional support that they require, so that they are able to make a successful transition from living in care to a more independent lifestyle.

Permanence – Refers to any arrangement under which children are likely to have continuous care throughout their childhood. This may be a return to their birth family, adoption, special guardianship, long-term foster care or another suitable arrangement.

Personal adviser – Connexions personal advisers provide information, advice and guidance, support for young people aged 13 to 19, including vulnerable young people requiring more substantial one-to-one support. Their key objective is to support young people to remain in learning and to fulfil their potential.

Personal Education Plan – An individual plan for looked-after-children developed in partnership with the child's school and which focuses on their educational needs, and is reviewed alongside the child's care plan.

Placement – In social care, placement refers to the physical living situation in which a child in care is 'placed' by the local authority; this reflects the wording used in the Children Act 1989. A placement may be with foster carers or in a residential children's home, for example.

Primary Care Trust – Primary care trusts (PCTs) are local free-standing NHS statutory bodies, responsible for planning, providing and commissioning health services for the local population. The government sees PCTs as the cornerstone of the NHS. Established under the provisions of the Health Act 1999, they provide all local GP, community and primary care services, and commission hospital services from other NHS trusts.

PSA – Public Service Agreements (PSAs) are three year agreements, negotiated between each of the main Departments and HM Treasury which set out a Department's high-level aims, priority objectives and key outcome-based performance targets.

Residential care – Refers to a type of placement in which the child lives in a children's home and is cared for by professional carers. The home must be registered with the Commission for Social care Inspection.

SEN – The Education Act 1996 defines a pupil as having a special educational need if he or she has 'a learning difficulty which calls for special educational provision to be made for him'. For the purposes of the Act, children are defined as having a learning difficulty if they: Have a significantly greater difficulty in learning than most children of the same age; Have a disability that prevents or hinders them from making use of educational facilities generally provided for children of the same age; or are under compulsory school age and would be likely to fall within one of the above definitions if special provision was not made for them.

Special guardianship – A Special Guardianship Order gives carers, such as grandparents or existing foster parents, clear responsibility for all aspects of caring for the child or young person, and for taking decisions to do with their upbringing. Special Guardianship preserves the basic legal link between the child or young person and their birth family, and is accompanied by proper access to a full range of support services.

Substance Misuse – The Updated National Drug Strategy and the *Every Child Matters* 'be healthy' outcome both use the term 'drugs' which refers to controlled drugs within the meaning of the Misuse of Drugs Act 1971. Reducing the use of these drugs by children and young people will often involve broader education, assessment and intervention covering a wider range of substances, including alcohol and volatile substances. Early use of these substances is a recognised risk factor for problem drug use in later life.

UASC – Unaccompanied Asylum Seeking Children are asylum seekers under the age of 18 who arrive in the country without a parent or guardian, many of whom will enter the care of local authorities as children in care.

Voluntary accommodation – This term is used to cover children who are in the care of a local authority under a voluntary agreement; in other words, children who are not the subject of a care order and for whom parental responsibility remains with the parents or primary carer. The legal basis for such children being looked after by the local authority are set out in section 20 of the Children Act 1989; because these arrangements are voluntary, accommodation agreements can be terminated by parents (or other person with parental responsibility) at any time.

Annex C
Key Data

C.1 A wide range of data are collected in relation to the children in care. This annex sets out key data from the "Children looked after by local authorities" collection (the SSDA 903 collection) and Outcome Indicators for Looked After Children" (the OC2 collection).

The population of children in care

C.2 There were 60,900 children in care on 31 March 2005. As the chart below illustrates, the number of children in care has risen over the past decade by approximately 10,000. This is due to an increase in the number of children in care on care orders.

Number of children with care orders or voluntary arrangements, 1995–2005

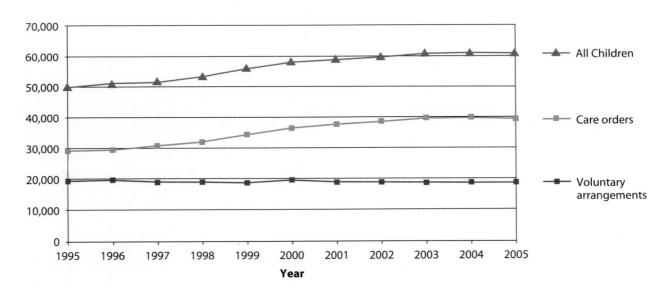

C.3 Children in care are a diverse group and the two charts below illustrate the age and race of children in care.

Age of children in care at 31 March 2005

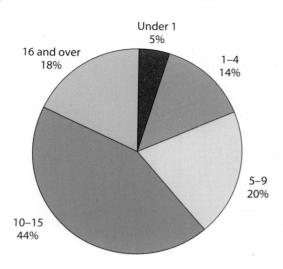

Race/ethnicity of children in care at 31 March 2005

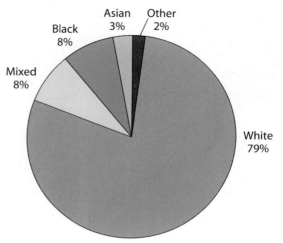

C.4 Local authorities record the primary reason for a child coming into care – 63% come into care because of abuse or neglect.

Primary reason for coming into care: children in care at 31 March 2005

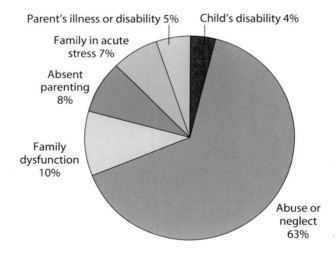

Children's experience of care

C.5 The average length of time spent in care by a child who left care in 2004/05 was 781 days – 2 years and 51 days. This has increased gradually from 712 days in 2001.

C.6 The legal status of a child has a significant impact on how long they stay in care. Children in care under care orders are likely to spend much longer in care than those in care on a voluntary basis. This is illustrated in the chart overleaf.

Percentage breakdown of duration of latest period of care by legal status (2004-05)

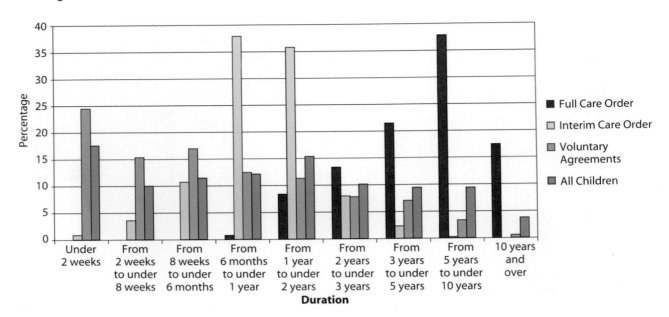

C.7 There are a range of different types of placement for children in care – the majority (68%) live with foster carers. The chart below describes the proportions of children in care living in different types of placement on 31 March 2005.

Proportion of children in care by type of placement, 31 March 2005

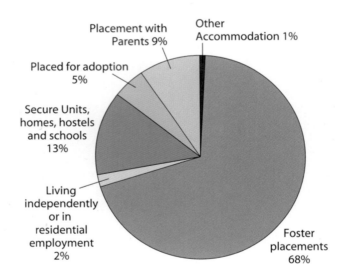

C.8 We know that stability is a very important issue for children in care. In particular, we know that instability will increase the likelihood of a child not achieving good educational outcomes. The chart below identifies the proportion of children of different ages who were in 3 or more placements in 2004/05.

Children with 3 or more placement during the year ending 31 March 2005 by age

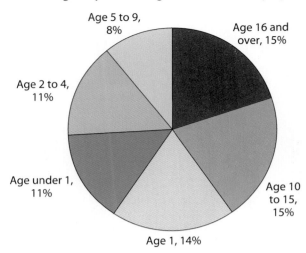

Adoption of children in care

C.9   Since the Prime Minister's initiative on adoption in 2000, 3,900 more children have been adopted than would have been the case if adoption remained at 1999-2000 levels. The charts below set out the age and race of children adopted in 2004/05.

Age breakdown of children in care placed for adoption at 31 March 2005

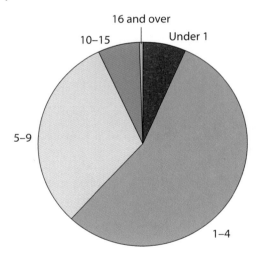

Children in care adopted during year ending 31 March 2005, by race/ethnicity

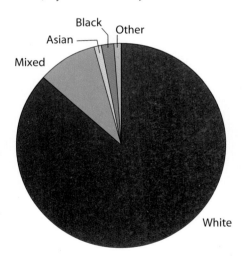

Outcomes for children in care

EDUCATION

C.10   Although the GCSE achievement of children in care has improved over the past few years, it has not improved at the same rate as other children. As a result, the gap in attainment has widened slightly. This is illustrated by the graphs below.

Percentage of children in care in Year 11 and all children aged 15 sitting at least one GNVQ examination

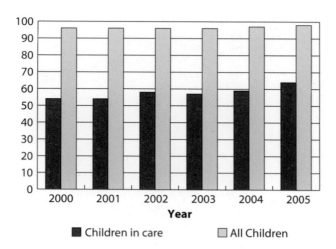

Percentage of children in care in Year 11 and all children aged 15 achieving at least 5 GCSE or GNVQ examinations at grades A*–G

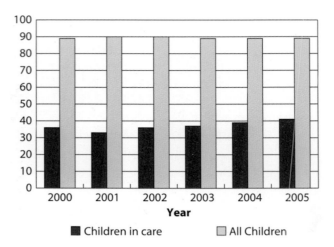

Percentage of children in care in Year 11 and all children aged 15 achieving at least one GCSE or GNVQ examination

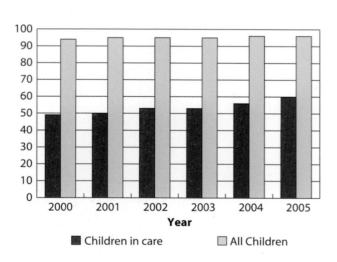

Percentage of children in care in Year 11 and all children aged 15 achieving at least 5 GCSE or GNVQ examinations at grades A*–C

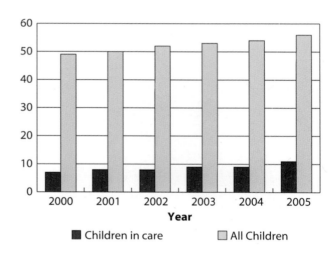

C.11 We know that young people's experience of care has a direct impact on their attainment. For example, if children come into care in the year before their GCSE exams, they are less likely to achieve 5 good GCSEs.

Attainment of care leavers with opportunity of sitting examinations before leaving by duration of their latest period of care

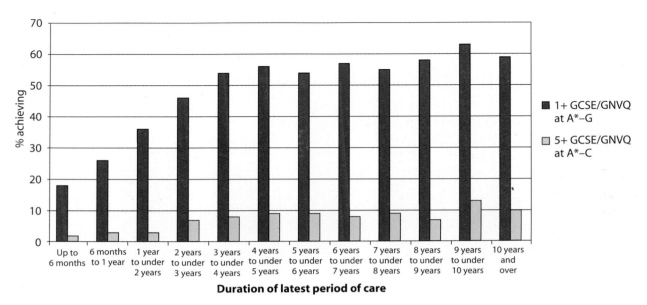

C.12 Similarly, the educational outcomes of children in care differ significantly by type of placement – children in foster care are more likely to achieve 5 good GCSEs than children in residential care. However, it is important to note that more vulnerable children with more complex needs are often placed in residential care.

GCSE attainment by type of placement during year ending 31 March 2005

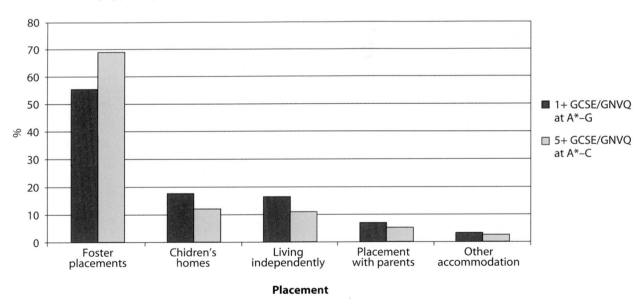

C.13 One of the most significant barriers to children in care achieving is the instability and upheaval caused by moving placement. It is important to note that analysis also shows that for all children changing school, particularly in years 10 and 11, can be a significant barrier to academic achievement.

C.14 Children in care have higher rates of exclusion than other children.

Percentage of children permanently excluded from school, 2000–2005

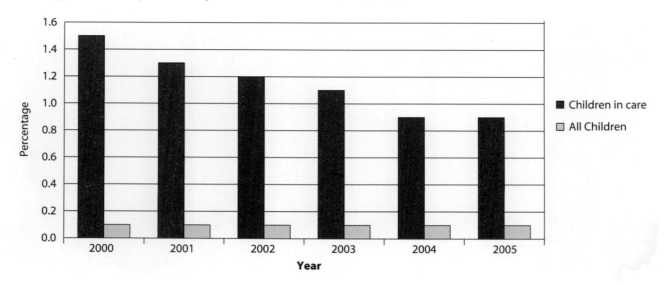

HEALTH

C.15 The proportion of children in care receiving their annual health check, dental check up and immunisations has improved year on year since this data was first collected.

Health care of children in care, twelve months ending 30 September 2000 to 2005

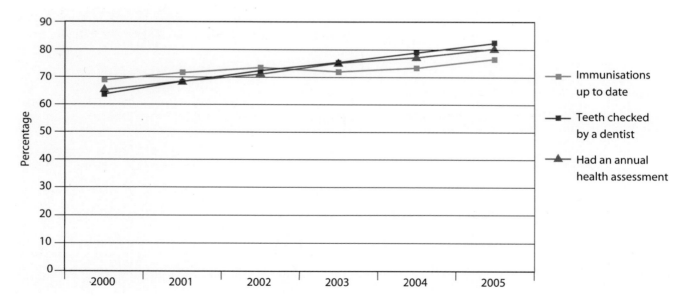

OFFENDING

C.16 Children in care are more likely to receive a warning, reprimand or conviction than other young people.

Proportion of children receiving a warning, reprimand or conviction, 2000–2005

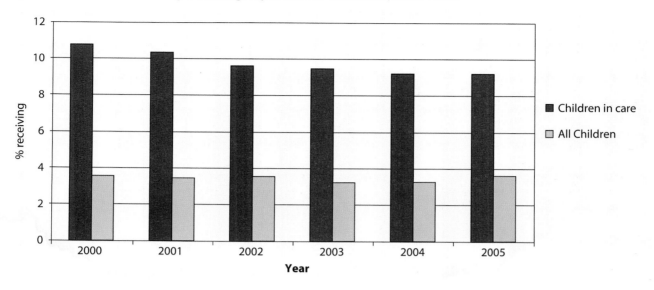

Care leavers

C.17 Since the introduction of the Children (Leaving Care) Act 2000, the age profile of young people leaving care aged 16 or over has changed considerably, with the proportion of young people leaving care at 16 decreasing significantly and the proportion continuing in care until 18 increasing.

Proportion of care leavers leaving at ages 16, 17 and 18 year ending 31 March 1995 to 2005

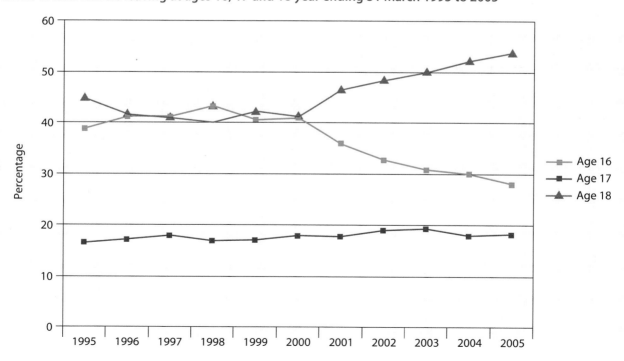

C.18 Over the same period the proportion of care leavers remaining in touch with their local authority and participating in education, employment and training has increased year on year.

Comparison between care leavers, aged 19, and all young people at age 19, not in education, employment or training between 2002 and 2005

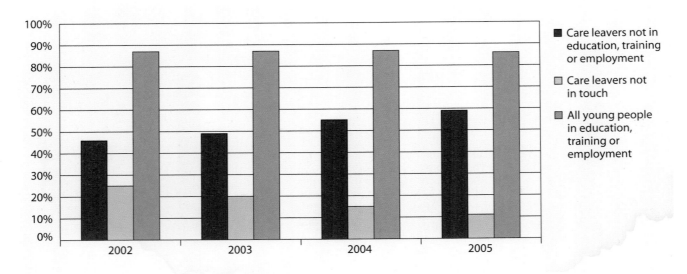

C.19 Over the same period, the proportion of care leavers aged 19 participating in university and education has risen.

Participation of care leavers, aged 19, in education between 2002 and 2005

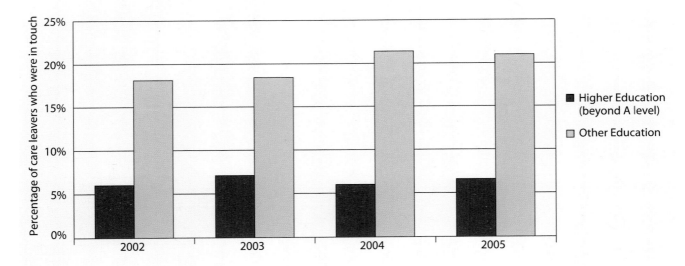

Printed in the UK for The Stationery Office Limited
on behalf of the Controller of Her Majesty's Stationery Office
ID5447728   10/06   JW4524

Printed on Paper containing 75% post consumer waste and 25% ECF pulp.